A BRIEF HISTORY OF ANNE FRANK

Unravelling a Tale of Courage and Survival in the Holocaust and World War II

SCOTT MATTHEWS

Copyright © 2024 Scott Matthews

All rights reserved. No part of this publication may be reproduced, distributed or transmitted in any form or by any means, including photocopying, recording, or other electronic or mechanical methods, without the prior written permission of the publisher, except in the case of brief quotations embodied in critical reviews and certain other non-commercial uses permitted by copyright law.

Trademarked names appear throughout this book. Rather than use a trademark symbol with every occurrence of a trademarked name, names are used in an editorial fashion, with no intention of infringement of the respective owner's trademark. The information in this book is distributed on an "as is" basis, without warranty. Although every precaution has been taken in the preparation of this work, neither the author nor the publisher shall have any liability to any person or entity with respect to any loss or damage caused or alleged to be caused directly or indirectly by the information contained in this book.

Contents

Introduction	vii
The World Before the Storm	1
The Frank Family: Origins and Early Life	7
Rising Tensions	13
Flight to Amsterdam	19
Shadows Over Europe	29
Into Hiding: The Secret Annex	37
The Annex: A Microcosm of Hope and Resilience	43
Anne's World Within Walls	53
Betrayal and Capture	63
The Final Days	71
The Diary Lives On	76
Legacy and Memory	83
The Betrayal of the Frank Family	88
The Holocaust: Beyond the Secret Annex	92
Reflections on Humanity and Hope	101
Conclusion	107
Appendix	111
References	117

"In spite of everything, I still believe that people are really good at heart."

- Anne Frank

Introduction

In the shadow of a war-torn past and on the cusp of yet another global upheaval, the early 20th century was a time of drastic change and uncertainty in Europe. It was against this background of turmoil and transformation that Anne Frank's story unfolded – a narrative that would come to symbolize the enduring strength of the human spirit in the middle of the darkest times. The book *A Brief History of Anne Frank* seeks to unveil the complexities of the world that shaped the lives of Anne and countless others, delving into the socio-political upheavals that preceded World War II and the subsequent events that led to the Holocaust.

Our journey begins in the aftermath of World War I, a conflict that left Europe fragmented and stumbling. The Treaty of Versailles, with its aim of securing lasting peace, instead sowed the seeds of resentment and economic hardship, particularly in Germany. The strict laws of compensation for their part in World War I and territorial losses put on the nation not only crippled its economy but also gave rise to a sense of injustice and humiliation among its people. This period of instability set the stage for the rise of extremist ideologies, marking the beginning of a dark chapter in history.

As we explore the world before the storm, we witness the interplay of economic distress, and the political and social change that characterized the interwar years. From the Roaring Twenties to the devastating impact of the Great Depression, these tumultuous times created a fertile ground for the rise of totalitarian regimes. Among this landscape of shifting power and emerging threats, a young girl named Anne Frank was born, destined to become one of history's most poignant voices.

Through this book, I aim to provide not just a recounting of historical events and Anne Frank's life but a deeper understanding of the era that Anne Frank was born into – a time fraught with challenges but also filled with the potential for resilience and hope. Her diary, a testament to the struggles and dreams of a young life cut tragically short, offers a window into the human experiences that define and transcend the collective past of the world. Join me as we trace the journey of Anne Frank and her family, from the early years of promise and potential through the darkness of the Holocaust, and reflect on the lessons that her story continues to teach us today.

The World Before the Storm

In the years leading up to World War II, Europe was a continent on the brink, grappling with the aftershocks of World War I (1914-1918) and the vast economic upheaval of the Great Depression. This period, rich in political and social change, set the stage for the emergence of one of history's most poignant and important voices: Anne Frank. Her story, and the world she was born into, is a testimony to the resilience of the human spirit in the face of burgeoning darkness.

Central to this era's legacy was the Treaty of Versailles, signed in 1919, a pivotal document meant to establish a lasting peace following the devastating impacts of World War I. Made by the victors of World War I, particularly France, the United Kingdom, and the United States, its primary aim was to prevent Germany from ever becoming a military threat again. However, the treaty went beyond merely setting military limitations; it placed heavy financial burdens on Germany through reparations - payments intended to compensate the Allies for the immense costs of the war.

These reparations were set at levels far beyond Germany's ability to pay, thus increasing the nation's economic woes. Germany was required to give significant territories to neighboring countries, lose all of its overseas colonies, and limit the size and capabilities of its military forces. This reduction in national sovereignty and economic power led to widespread poverty among the German population, who felt unfairly punished by terms they saw as excessively harsh and humiliating.

This pervasive atmosphere of humiliation and despair did not just strain Germany's post-war recovery; it created a fertile ground for extremist ideologies to flourish. The harshness of the Treaty of Versailles unintentionally fostered a sense of injustice and betrayal among Germans, contributing to a nationalistic backlash. It was within this context of economic instability and national humiliation that radical movements found their voice, promising to restore Germany's pride and status. The treaty, intended to secure peace, thus became a catalyst for further conflict, laying the foundational grievances that would eventually fuel the rise of Adolf Hitler and the Nazi Party, leading the world once again into a devastating global conflict.

As the 1920s dawned, Europe experienced a fleeting period of economic recovery and cultural vibrancy known as the Roaring Twenties. Technological advancements and a booming entertainment industry brought jazz, cinema, and a sense of optimism. Yet, this prosperity was not universally felt. In rural areas and among the working class, the scars of war remained deep, and economic disparity became even more pronounced.

The Wall Street Crash of 1929, often referred to as the Great Crash, was a catastrophic financial event that marked the start of the Great Depression, a decade-long period of economic downturn that affected  industrialized countries worldwide. Beginning in late October of that year, over the course of several days known collectively as "Black Thursday," "Black Monday," and "Black Tuesday," the stock market on Wall Street in New York City saw a dramatic and unprecedented decline. This collapse was marked by a rapid fall in stock prices, leading to massive financial losses for investors. The crash not only wiped out millions of dollars of wealth almost overnight but also led to the decline of public confidence in the economy. As a direct consequence, consumer spending and investment dropped sharply, leading to a severe economic contraction. Banks failed, businesses closed, and unemployment rates soared, marking the onset of the deepest and most widespread economic depression of the 20th century. Europe, heavily reliant on American loans, was hit hard by this. Unemployment soared, banks collapsed, and social unrest became commonplace. In Germany, this dire economic situation helped propel Adolf Hitler and his National Socialist (Nazi) Party to power. Promising to revive the economy and restore German pride, Hitler's rise to chancellor in 1933 marked a dark turn toward authoritarian rule.

Fascism, a political ideology characterized by authoritarian nationalism and the suppression of opposition, found a stronghold not only in Germany but also in Italy under Benito Mussolini. These regimes glorified the state over the individual, pursued aggressive expansionism,[1] and fostered a

---

1. Expansionism is a policy adopted by states or nations to expand their territory, influence, or economic dominance through various means, including military conquest, colonization, or diplomatic agreements. This policy is often

cult of personality around their leaders. Meanwhile, the Soviet Union under Joseph Stalin embarked on a different but equally oppressive path, aiming to transform the agrarian (agricultural) society into an industrial powerhouse through rapid industrialization. These efforts, while modernizing the Soviet economy, resulted in the suffering and deaths of millions.

The Spanish Civil War, which took place from 1936 to 1939, was a major event that showed just how divided Europe had become in terms of beliefs and politics. This war in Spain was essentially a fight between two groups: on one side were the Nationalists, led by General Francisco Franco, who had strong conservative and fascist views, supported by countries like Nazi Germany and Fascist Italy. On the other side were the Republicans, who wanted to keep the government democratic and progressive, with support from the Soviet Union and international volunteers who believed in fighting against fascism.

This war wasn't just a conflict within Spain but became a battleground for larger, competing ideas that were spreading across Europe. The Nationalists, with their fascist backing, believed in a strong, centralized government and often suppressed any opposition or dissent. The Republicans, however, supported the idea of democracy and freedom of speech, and were generally more left-leaning, looking to the Soviet Union for support against the rising tide of fascism, which is a system where power is held by one leader or party, often controlling people's lives with strict rules and no opposition is allowed. Franco's victory in the war not only established a dictatorial regime in Spain but also signaled the strength and appeal of fascist ideologies in Europe at the time. It showed how the continent was becoming more militarized,

---

driven by a desire for more resources, strategic advantages, economic benefits, or a belief in the nation's superiority or manifest destiny.

meaning countries were building up their armies and preparing for potential conflict.

Beneath the political upheaval, societal changes were afoot. The interwar years saw significant shifts in the role of women, who, having stepped into the workforce during World War I, began to challenge traditional gender roles and advocate for greater rights, including suffrage, which means fighting for women's right to vote in political elections. Culturally, the period was marked by a quest for meaning in the wake of the devastation of World War I. Artistic movements sought to weaken established norms and explore the subconscious, reflecting the disillusionment of the era. The advent of talking pictures transformed cinema into a powerful medium of mass entertainment and propaganda, offering an escape from the grim realities of the day.

As Europe edged closer to war, the societal landscape was marked by contrasts – between the vibrancy of cultural expression and the darkening political horizon and between advancements in technology and the rise of totalitarian regimes. This complex environment of political extremism, economic turmoil, and social change shaped the early years of Anne Frank's life and would come to define the world into which she would step as one of history's most enduring voices. Her diary, an emblem of hope and resilience amidst the darkest of times, offers a deeply personal glimpse into the human costs of war and the indomitable spirit of those who lived through it.

The story of Europe before World War II is thus one of contrasts – of brightness and shadow, progress and regression, hope and despair. It is within this tumultuous landscape that the life and legacy of Anne Frank take on profound significance, reminding us of the light that can emerge from even the darkest of times.

The Frank Family: Origins and Early Life

Before the world was engulfed in the shadows of war, the Frank family led a life rich in culture, intellect, and the spirit of resilience, much like many Jewish families in early 20th-century Europe. In the heart of Frankfurt, Germany, the Franks had made a home filled with laughter, learning, and a deep connection to both tradition and the bustling world around them.

At the center of this vibrant family life was Anne Frank, born Annelies Marie on June 12, 1929, to her loving parents, Otto and Edith Frank. Otto Heinrich Frank, the family patriarch, was born into a world of commerce and tradition in 1889. His lineage was steeped in the banking profession, with his family being well-respected members of the Frankfurt Jewish community. Otto himself was a man of sophistication and ambition, qualities that would guide him through the trials of his later life. The valor of Anne's father and uncle Robert during World War I, where they served as German officers, underlined the family's long-standing loyalty and contributions to their country. Additionally, Anne's grandmother's service as a nurse in a military hospital during the same conflict exemplified the family's dedication to aiding those in need amidst the turmoil of war.

Edith Holländer Frank, born in 1900, brought her own distinguished heritage into the family. Coming from an affluent German-Jewish family in Aachen, Edith was raised in a household that valued education and cultural enrichment, much like the one she would create with Otto. Their union in 1925 was not just a merging of hearts but of two rich cultural and intellectual lineages, setting the foundation for the family they would build together. Otto Frank wed Edith Holländer when he was a mature thirty-six, and she, a vibrant twenty-five.

Alongside her sister Margot who was three years her senior, Anne grew up in an environment where education was celebrated, curiosity was encouraged, and diversity was embraced. Otto and Edith, who themselves came from Jewish German backgrounds, were determined to safely raise their daughters in a world that was starting to change, sometimes in unsettling ways.

In the Frank family's early days, the contrast between Otto and Edith Frank's personalities significantly shaped their home life. Otto, noticeably older and outgoing, was the heart of their household's energy and joy. His storytelling and photography were not just hobbies but ways to connect deeply with his daughters, Anne and Margot. They affectionately called him Pim, a nickname that symbolized their close bond. Edith, more reserved and quiet, provided a stabilizing force, balancing Otto's enthusiasm with her calm presence.

The stories Otto shared, particularly about two fictional sisters, both, named Paula, mirrored his daughters' personalities. Margot was the epitome of the well-behaved Paula, while Anne identified with the adventurous one, highlighting her spirited and mischievous nature. This storytelling tradition became a cherished part of their family life. Moreover, Anne's relationship with her grandmother, Oma, brought additional warmth to her childhood. Oma's doting nature and Anne's outspokenness led to amusing and memorable moments. Once, on a bus journey with Oma, Anne, at just four and a half years old, scanned the crowded space and boldly exclaimed, "Won't someone offer a seat to this old lady?" This early episode in Anne's life perfectly captures her forthright nature. Even as a young child, Anne didn't hesitate to speak her mind, showcasing the outspoken character that would define her as she grew older.

Initially, after Anne and Margot were born, the family resided at Marbachweg 307 in the Frankfurt-Dornbusch area, where they rented two floors. This neighborhood that was distinguished by its tranquil streets and sense of community provided a stable and nurturing environment for the young family. The family's house on Marbachweg, chosen for its affordability and the promise of a touch of nature that Edith wanted for her children, marked a departure from the urban elite Jewish circles Otto and Edith were used to. However, this relocation to a neighborhood primarily inhabited by civil servants and professionals other than businessmen, like Otto, offered a new perspective and perhaps a more diverse social environment for the growing family.

The early years in Marbachweg proved beneficial for young Margot, and later Anne, offering a semblance of an idyllic, small-town existence. Their home had separate living quarters connected by a staircase and was perfectly adapted to their needs. It housed not just the family's extensive library, indicating Otto and Edith's broad intellectual interests, but also spaces that catered to personal pursuits, such as Edith's study.

When the Franks moved to Marbachweg, Gertrud Naumann, a ten-year-old girl and next-door neighbor, quickly became a cherished part of their family. With her thick blonde braids and friendly grin, she displayed a natural curiosity and warmth toward the Frank family from the moment their moving van arrived. The youngest among six siblings, Gertrud had a profound affinity for babies, enthusiastically engaging with Margot by pushing her around in the baby carriage and introducing her to the neighborhood kids. Despite being a child herself, Gertrud exhibited a sense of responsibility and care beyond her years, qualities that Edith Frank recognized and appreciated, entrusting Margot's care to her with confidence.

Gertrud's relationship with the Frank family extended beyond that of a mere babysitter or a playmate for the children. She was integrated into their daily lives, often joining them for meals and becoming a fixture in their home. Gertrud's presence brought additional joy and vitality to the household, sharing in the Franks' culinary experiences, from enjoying Edith's stews to indulging in bowls of cornflakes with apple and cream – a delicacy unique to the Franks' table. Despite Edith's upbringing in a kosher,[1] the Frank family's dietary practices were adapted to be inclusive, ensuring that meals were a communal and welcoming experience for guests like Gertrud, irrespective of their religious backgrounds.

---

1. Kosher is a term used to describe food that complies with the strict dietary standards of traditional Jewish law. For many Jews, kosher is about more than just health or food safety. It is about reverence and adherence to religious tradition.

Over time, Gertrud's bond with the Frank family deepened, transcending the typical boundaries between a family and their guest. She was treated almost as a daughter, with Otto Frank affectionately being referred to as "Papa Frank" by her. The Franks regarded Gertrud as part of their family, evident in the thoughtful gifts they gave her and her inclusion in family vacations, such as their trip to Bad Soden. This affection was warmly reciprocated by Gertrud, who also considered the Franks her family

Seeking more space and perhaps a reflection of their growing aspirations, the Franks later moved to a more fashionable area of Dornbusch, the Poets' Quarter (Dichterviertel). By 1931, they had settled into their new home at Ganghoferstraße 24. This area, known for its liberal atmosphere and intellectual vibrancy, was fitting for a family deeply engaged in scholarly and cultural pursuits. The Dichterviertel, with its leafy streets and elegant homes, was a hub for Frankfurt's intellectual community, offering the Franks a stimulating environment for both personal and intellectual growth. The move to their new home was prompted by economic necessity and perhaps a search for a more welcoming community amidst rising anti-Semitism. Yet, their bond with Gertrud remained strong even in their new home, where she occasionally came to meet.

The Franks were the kind of family who blended their Jewish heritage with a more liberal outlook, identifying as liberal Jews. This open-minded approach to life was reflected in their participation in a community where Jews and non-Jews mingled freely. This openness and acceptance were the bedrock of Anne and Margot's upbringing, teaching them the value of understanding and tolerance from a young age.

A love for books and the arts was a gift Otto and Edith passed down to their daughters. Their home was a treasure trove of books, encouraging Anne and Margot to explore worlds beyond their own. This foundation of knowledge and empathy would later become a source of strength for Anne, helping her voice resonate through her diary. The Frank sisters' education and upbringing were a reflection of a broader cultural commitment to scholarship and the arts, typical of many families in their social circle.

Anne and Margot shared the special bond of siblings – full of fun and occasional squabbles, but always underpinned by love. Anne looked up to her father, Otto, as her guide and protector, while her relationship with her mother, Edith, was more complex, filled with the highs and lows that mark the journey from childhood to adolescence.

In those early days, the Franks enjoyed the comfort and security of their home, unaware of the tumultuous times ahead. Their story is a touching reminder of the simple joys and normalcy that existed for many families before the storm of war – a time that would become a precious memory for those who survived and a profound loss for those who did not.

Rising Tensions

In 20th-century history, few events are as dark or as significant as the rise of Adolf Hitler and the Nazi Party in Germany. This period, marked by escalating tensions and the spread of anti-Semitic policies, profoundly impacted the lives of Jewish families across Europe, including the Franks. As the clouds of conflict gathered, the Frank family, like so many others, found their world turned upside down, setting the stage for a chapter in their lives filled with uncertainty and fear.

The early 1930s in Germany witnessed not only economic hardship and political instability but also a profound social upheaval. The Treaty of Versailles, which had concluded World War I, imposed harsh reparations on Germany, severely crippling its economy. This financial burden, coupled with the global impact of the Great Depression that began in 1929, plunged the country into deep economic despair. Unemployment soared, reaching unprecedented levels, and inflation rendered the German currency nearly worthless, eroding the savings of the middle class and creating widespread poverty.

Amidst this chaos, Adolf Hitler and the National Socialist German Workers' Party (Nazi Party) found fertile ground for their ideology. The Nazis adeptly manipulated the widespread discontent, attributing Germany's misfortunes to the Weimar Republic's democratic government, which was Germany's government from 1919 to 1933, the period after World War I until the rise of Nazi power. The Nazi party claimed the Weimar government was both incompetent and corrupt while propagating virulent anti-Semitic rhetoric and expressing hostility toward foreigners, blaming Jews and other minorities for the nation's economic woes and promoting the idea of racial purity.

Hitler's charismatic leadership and the Nazi Party's promises of economic revival, restoration of national pride, and expansion of territory resonated with a population desperate for change. The Nazis used propaganda effectively, employing modern technology and mass media to spread their message. Rallies, speeches, and parades showcased Hitler's public speaking skills and the party's strength, appealing to nationalistic and militaristic sentiments.

The Nazi Party's rise was also facilitated by the failure of the Weimar Republic's political parties to unite against this growing threat. The fragmented political landscape, marked by short-lived coalitions and constant infighting, made it difficult to stage an effective opposition. Additionally, the economic elite, fearing the rise of communism[1] more than

---

1. Communism is a political and economic ideology that seeks to create a classless society in which the major means of production, such as mines, factories, and farms, are owned and controlled by the public or the state.

fascism, saw Hitler as a protection against the leftist ideology and, therefore, provided financial support to the Nazi Party.

By exploiting the public's fears and frustrations, the Nazis gained substantial support in the early 1930s. Their breakthrough came in the 1932 elections, where they emerged as the largest party in the Reichstag, Germany's parliament. Though initially not in a majority, this position allowed Hitler to demand the chancellorship, which he was appointed to on January 30, 1933. Once in power, Hitler and the Nazis moved quickly to consolidate their control, transforming Germany into a totalitarian state.

The Enabling Act, officially known as the "Law to Remedy the Distress of the People and the Reich," was passed on March 23, 1933, and it played a pivotal role in the establishment of Adolf Hitler's dictatorship in Germany.  This legislation was crucial for Hitler's consolidation of power as it allowed him to enact laws, including those altering the constitution, without the approval of the Reichstag (the German Parliament) or the German President.

The introduction of the Enabling Act was a direct assault on the Weimar Constitution, which had established Germany as a democratic republic following World War I. The Weimar Constitution provided for a balance of power, ensuring that legislative authority rested with the Reichstag and the Reichsrat and that the President had limited emergency powers. However, with the Enabling Act in place, Hitler could bypass these democratic institutions and legislate alone and without any other authority.

To pass the Enabling Act, a two-thirds majority vote in the Reichstag was required, a threshold Hitler managed to achieve through a combination of political maneuvering and intimidation. The atmosphere of fear and crisis was significantly amplified by the Reichstag Fire, an arson attack on the German parliament building on February 27, 1933. This event was pivotal, as the Nazis claimed it was a communist plot to overthrow the state, thus justifying the arrest and suppression of their political opponents, especially the communists. The Nazi Party, lacking a sufficient majority on its own, exploited the situation to its advantage. With the Communist Party's members already prohibited from taking their seats due to the Reichstag Fire Decree – a legislative response to the fire that suspended many civil liberties and allowed for the arrest of political adversaries – Hitler found it easier to diminish opposition. This context of orchestrated emergency and the direct aftermath of the Reichstag Fire enabled Hitler to convince and coerce enough members of other parties into compliance to secure the necessary vote for the Enabling Act. This act effectively dismantled the Weimar Republic's democratic governance, granting Hitler and his cabinet the power to enact laws without the need for parliamentary consent, marking the beginning of the authoritarian rule of the Third Reich.

Once enacted, the Enabling Act effectively nullified the checks and balances that were the hallmark of a democratic system. It allowed Hitler and his cabinet to enact laws, including those that contradicted the Weimar Constitution, without any parliamentary review or debate. This act marked the end of democratic governance in Germany and the transition to a totalitarian rule. It laid the legal foundation for the Nazi regime to implement its agenda without opposition, leading to the systematic suppression of freedoms, the persecution of political opponents, Jews, and other minorities, and ultimately, to World War II and the Holocaust. The Enabling Act represented the legal transformation of the Weimar Republic into the Third Reich, giving Hitler the disguise of legality for his actions, despite the profound undemocratic nature of his regime.

For the Frank family, this rising tide of anti-Semitism was both shocking and bewildering. Otto and Edith Frank, who had embraced the values of enlightenment, with pursuits of knowledge, and assimilation in the rising modern world, suddenly found themselves and their children marginalized in their own country. The Nuremberg Laws of 1935, which stripped Jews of their citizenship and forbade marriage or sexual relations between Jews and non-Jewish Germans, were a stark indication of the worsening situation. Jewish businesses, including those owned by families like the Franks, faced boycotts, vandalism, and increasing legal restrictions, systematically dismantling their means of livelihood.

The impact on daily life was immediate and distressing. Margot and Anne, who had once moved freely and joyfully in their neighborhood, now faced exclusion from public schools, parks, and swimming pools. Friendships were strained or broken as non-Jewish families, either out of fear or indoctrination of Nazi's hatred, distanced themselves from their Jewish neighbors. The vibrant community life that the Franks had cherished was disintegrating, replaced by a climate of fear and suspicion.

The propaganda machine of the Nazi regime, meanwhile, worked tirelessly to dehumanize the Jewish population. Newspapers, radio broadcasts, and public speeches painted Jews as the root of Germany's problems, cementing anti-Semitic attitudes in the minds of the population. This constant bombardment of hatred served not only to justify the regime's policies but also to isolate Jews further, making it difficult for them to find allies or support among the non-Jewish German population.

Despite these adversities, the Frank family attempted to maintain a semblance of normality. Otto and Edith worked tirelessly to shield Anne and Margot from the worst of the hatred, striving to preserve the warmth and love that had always characterized their home. They reinforced the importance of education, encouraging the girls to read widely and continue learning despite being banned from attending school. Otto, with his deep love for German culture and his faith in human decency, hoped for a time when the madness would end and reason would prevail.

However, as the situation in Germany worsened, such hopes started to seem increasingly naive. The Kristallnacht pogrom of November 1938, during which Jewish synagogues, businesses, and homes were attacked across the country, was a terrifying demonstration of the Nazi regime's capacity for violence. For the Franks and countless other Jewish families, it was a clear signal that they were no longer safe in Germany.

The early impact of anti-Semitism on the Franks was profound, marking the end of their peaceful life in Frankfurt and the beginning of a period of uncertainty and upheaval. Yet, through it all, the family's bond remained strong. They drew strength from each other and from the hope that, somehow, they would find a way to survive the dark times ahead.

As the shadows of war loomed larger and the Nazi regime's policies became increasingly aggressive, the Frank family, like so many others, were forced to make a decision. They would leave their home, their friends, and everything they knew in search of safety. This decision, fraught with uncertainty and danger, would set them on a path that would forever mark their place in history.

Flight to Amsterdam

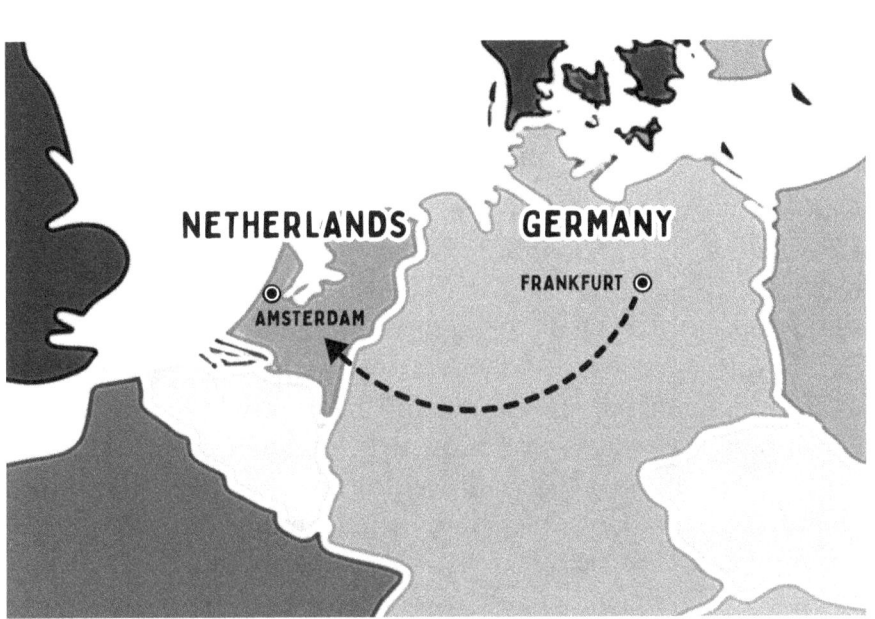

Under the expanding shadow of National Socialism across Germany, the vibrant and intellectually rich life once enjoyed by the Frank family in Frankfurt was increasingly scared by the ever-growing anti-Semitism of the era. This darkening atmosphere led to a pivotal moment for the Franks, forcing them to confront the grim reality of their situation. As they resettled in the Westend of Frankfurt, it became clear that their cherished way of life was under threat, encouraging a deep reflection on their future and the well-being of their daughters, Margot and Anne.

Margot, a thoughtful and introspective seven-year-old, faced immediate challenges as she transitioned to the Varrentrapp School. In the school, the National Socialist policies came even into the classroom. She was segregated from her non-Jewish classmates and subjected to the ideological biases of the time. Margot's experience was an indicator of the systemic exclusion that awaited Jewish children. This distressing situation, along with the growing likelihood that Anne, now of kindergarten age, would also be secluded from public education, deeply concerned Otto and Edith. The rising restrictions on Jewish life in Germany highlighted the urgent need for the Frank family to find refuge in a place where their daughters could grow and learn free from persecution.

The resolve to leave their homeland was further solidified on May 10, 1933, when National Socialist student groups staged public book burnings across Germany. This act was aimed at removing "un-German" elements from cultural life and was a harrowing spectacle that laid open the regime's hostility toward intellectual freedom and diversity. The fire that consumed the works of renowned Jewish authors not only represented an attack on cultural heritage but also served as a chilling omen of the violence to come. Among the condemned authors was Heinrich Heine, a poet cherished by Otto and known to German schoolchildren, whose works were now erased from the national consciousness. Additionally, Heine's prophetic insight that the burning of books would pave the way for the burning of people was tragically unfolding into reality.

Faced with these difficult circumstances, Otto and Edith were driven by a determination to shield their daughters from the rising climate of hate and to preserve the core of their family's identity. Their decision to emigrate, filled with uncertainty, was underpinned by a hope for a safer, more tolerant environment. For the Franks, Amsterdam emerged as a potential refuge, offering the promise of a fresh start away from the shadows that had fallen over their lives in Frankfurt.

Amsterdam in the 1930s was a bustling metropolis known for its liberal attitudes and cultural diversity. It was this reputation that drew Otto Frank to the city in the summer of 1933. He initially went to Amsterdam alone to lay the groundwork for his family's new life. Otto's familiarity with the Dutch language already put him at an advantage, easing his transition and aiding in the establishment of their new beginning in Amsterdam. The Netherlands had a long-standing tradition of religious tolerance, and Amsterdam, in particular, had been a refuge for Jewish people during periods of persecution throughout history. Otto's move was a leap of faith, fueled by the hope that Amsterdam would offer his family safety and the freedom to live without fear.

Upon his arrival, Otto began the difficult task of establishing a new business. He eventually set up Opekta, a company that sold pectin, a substance used for making jam. It was a venture that would not only provide for his  family but also become a significant part of the Frank family's life in Amsterdam, particularly the Secret Annex above the Opekta offices where they would later hide. In this period of transition, Edith Frank played a crucial role, journeying between Aachen and Amsterdam to secure a new home for her family. She discovered an apartment in Merwedeplein, located in the Rivierenbuurt neighborhood, an area that was becoming a sanctuary for Jewish-German refugees like themselves.

By November 1933, Edith had relocated to Amsterdam, followed closely by Margot. Anne remained with her grandmother until February 1934, when the family was finally reunited in their new Dutch home. Their move was part of a larger exodus, with the Franks among the approximately 300,000 Jews who fled Germany between 1933 and 1939, seeking safety from the oppressive reach of the Nazi regime.

In February 1934, Edith, Margot, and Anne joined Otto in Amsterdam, reuniting the family and marking the beginning of their new chapter. The transition was not without its challenges. Learning a new language and adapting to a different culture posed initial hurdles, but the Franks were embraced by their new community, and they quickly began to feel at home. Despite the geographical distance and the critical political climate in Germany, the Frank family made efforts to stay connected with their loved ones back in Frankfurt, including Gertrud. The bond they shared transcended the barriers imposed by the changing times, and the Franks diligently maintained these cherished relationships through the exchange of letters. This act of correspondence became a vital lifeline, a way to bridge the gap between Amsterdam and Frankfurt, keeping the warmth of their friendships alive despite the growing unrest and challenges of the era.

The family settled into a spacious apartment at Merwedeplein 37, in a quiet, leafy neighborhood. This area of Amsterdam was known for its intellectual and artistic residents, mirroring the Frank family's own values and interests. The family's integration into Dutch society was marked by the girls' progress in school and Otto's success with Opekta. Anne, in particular, showed a keen interest in language and writing, a talent that Edith and Otto encouraged. The cultural and intellectual stimulation that had been a hallmark of their life in Frankfurt continued in Amsterdam, with visits to museums, concerts, and lectures forming part of their regular activities.

In their new home, the vibrant and inquisitive Anne Frank found herself navigating a new chapter of her life in Amsterdam. Her fifth birthday marked not only a personal milestone but also the beginning of her journey in this new city, a transition marked by the excitement of making new friends and establishing a sense of normalcy in the middle of upheaval. Her lively nature and insatiable curiosity quickly endeared her to her peers, setting the stage for the creation of lasting bonds that would become a cornerstone of her life in Amsterdam.

On June 12, 1934, Anne's fifth birthday was celebrated with the joy and solidarity that had been an emblem of the Frank family's gatherings in Frankfurt. The move to Amsterdam had been a significant change for the family, especially for the young Anne, who thrived on interaction and was always eager to explore her surroundings. Despite the initial challenges of adapting to a new environment and the sting of separation from familiar faces in Frankfurt and Aachen, Anne's resilient spirit shone through.

Margot and Anne Frank were enrolled in local schools, with Margot attending a public school and Anne entering the sixth Montessori School. The Montessori school on Niersstraat became a new playground for Anne's curiosity and social endeavors. This institution would later honor Anne's legacy by adopting the name "Anne Frank School" in 1957. Despite facing initial challenges with the Dutch language, Margot quickly became an exemplary student, showcasing the family's commitment to education and excellence. Anne, on the other hand, found a sense of belonging and community at the Montessori school, where she formed friendships with peers, including Hanneli Goslar, who would become a cherished friend. Their friendship, rooted in shared language and experience, blossomed in their Montessori education, offering a sense of belonging and mutual understanding. Anne's circle of friends quickly expanded to include Sanne Ledermann and others, forming a tight-knit group that navigated the complexities of their new lives together.

Anne was an engaged student, though she had a strong aversion to mathematics. Her lively spirit often spilled over into her school days, where her inclination for chatting led to frequent reminders from her teachers to remain silent during lessons. Outside the classroom, Anne was brimming with energy and creativity, even founding a Ping-Pong club named "The Little Bear Minus 2 Club," which had five members. The peculiar name was inspired by Anne's mistaken count of stars in the Little Bear constellation; she thought there were five instead of seven, hence the "minus 2" in the club's name.

Another one of Anne's passions was reading. She devoured history texts and Greek myths, along with a beloved series about Joop, a spirited and adventurous girl much like Anne herself. Her adventurous spirit was matched by her physical activity; she was fond of ice skating and cycling, especially with her accomplice in mischief, Hanne. Together, they took part in playful pranks, including soaking people who walked by with water from the balcony of the Frank family apartment.

Anne, a competent swimmer, cherished the times she spent at the beach near Amsterdam, an experience vividly captured in photographs. These images show Anne and her sister Margot in their swimwear, fully enjoying the seaside. In one notable photograph, Anne appears shivering, wrapped in a blanket, which showcases her slender frame and underscores her mother's consistent concern for her health. This concern was not without reason, as Anne frequently suffered from health issues ranging from colds to the flu, which often required her absence from school.

Despite these health setbacks, Anne found solace and inspiration in the world of cinema. She regularly collected pictures of movie stars, and the allure of the silver screen fueled her fantasies of someday gaining fame herself. However, in the middle of her dreams of stardom, Anne often faced self-deprecating thoughts about her appearance, revealing a contrast between her aspirations and personal insecurities.

In Amsterdam, Otto and Edith recreated the nurturing, culturally rich environment that had defined their life in Frankfurt. Their home became a gathering place for friends and relatives, including fellow immigrants seeking refuge from

Germany. The sense of community and mutual support among these families was a source of strength and comfort.

In 1933, the River Quarter of Amsterdam had begun to transform as Jewish families, mainly immigrants fleeing the escalating persecution in Germany and later Austria, sought refuge in its reasonably priced accommodations. By the time the Frank family settled into their apartment on Merwedeplein, the neighborhood was still filling up. The shared experience of displacement and moving out from anti-Semitic places created a sense of unity among these immigrants, transcending previous social and cultural divides. The response of Dutch people to this influx of outsiders was mixed. They were initially open and welcoming but gradually there were people who started being overwhelmed by the newcomers.

Despite the language and cultural barriers, the Frank family, along with other German-speaking exiles, quickly made Amsterdam's South their own. The city's streetcars, frequently filled with German conversations, earned the nickname "Orient Express," a reminder of the presence and influence of the immigrant community. Despite some pushback from locals who saw a stark difference between Dutch citizens and German immigrants, Jewish or not, the newcomers were eager to become part of Dutch society. Their children, in particular, helped bridge this gap by quickly picking up the language and interacting with peers at school.

Otto and Edith Frank, keen to build a new life, forged connections with other exiled families, including the Goslars and the Ledermanns, who shared their suffering of displacement.

Hans Goslar, once a prominent government official in Prussia, a significant historical region that now forms part of Germany and Poland, found himself driven out due to his Jewish heritage even before Hitler's rise to power. Prussia, known for its influential role in shaping modern German statehood, became a challenging environment for many of its Jewish citizens during this period. Goslar's family's subsequent move to Amsterdam, seeking a temporary haven on their way to Palestine, mirrored the Franks' journey. Similarly, the Ledermanns, facing professional and social exclusion in Berlin, sought refuge in Amsterdam, where Franz Ledermann eventually resumed his legal career.

These families, though from diverse backgrounds, found common ground in their shared experience of displacement and hope for a safer future. The rituals of Jewish observance, especially the Sabbath ceremonies hosted by the Goslars, provided Edith Frank with a sense of continuity and spiritual solace in a foreign land. Despite Otto Frank's lack of religious upbringing, he respected these traditions, recognizing their significance to his wife and the broader community.

The immigrant families navigated the challenges of adaptation, from mastering the Dutch language to adjusting to new social norms. The women, in particular, struggled with the changes in their domestic lives, mourning the quality of local domestic help and longing for the familiarity of their lives in Germany. However, despite these challenges, the families strove to maintain their dignity and cultural identity, finding solace and strength in their tight-knit community as they faced an uncertain future together.

Otto Frank, ever industrious, founded a second company in 1938 named Pectacon, which specialized in the wholesale of herbs, pickling salts, and spices for sausage production. This venture brought Hermann van Pels into the Franks' lives, a Jewish butcher and spice advisor who, like them, had fled the escalating threats in Germany. The professional relationship between Otto and Hermann would later evolve into a deeper bond of trust and mutual support during the years of hiding.

For Anne and Margot, Amsterdam offered a freedom that had become increasingly restricted in Germany. They explored their new city with curiosity, taking particular delight in the canals, parks, and the vibrant street life. Anne, with her adventurous spirit, reveled in the city's history and culture, elements that would later be featured in her writing.

The family's sense of unity and security was further strengthened in 1939 when Edith Frank's mother joined them in Amsterdam. Her presence in the household until her passing in January 1942 provided additional comfort and continuity amidst the upheaval of relocation and the challenges of adapting to a new life in the Netherlands.

In their Rivierenbuurt home, the Franks embarked on a journey of rebuilding and adaptation. Their apartment on Merwedeplein became a symbol of hope and a fresh start, reflecting the broader narrative of Jewish refugees seeking safety and normalcy away from the persecution in Germany. This period was marked by a blend of personal growth, academic achievements, and the deepening of familial bonds as they navigated the complexities of their new environment.

Despite the semblance of stability and safety, the undercurrent of the growing conflict in Europe was never far from the minds of the Frank family. In 1938, a distressing event unfolded for Anne's family when her uncle, Walter, was arrested in Germany, solely due to his Jewish identity. He was confined to a labor camp, a place with conditions like those of a prison. Fortunately, Uncle Walter managed to secure his release by consenting to leave Germany permanently, a decision that ultimately led him to start a new life in the United States. This news from Germany, with the escalating persecution of Jews and the march toward war, was a constant reminder of what the Franks had fled. Yet, in these early years in Amsterdam, the Franks found a measure of peace and the opportunity to look forward with hope.

However, this period of relative tranquility was short-lived. In May 1940, the German army invaded the Netherlands, shattering any illusion of safety the Frank family might have harbored. The move to Amsterdam, initially seen as a flight toward freedom, became a prelude to the years of hiding that lay ahead. The city that had offered a new home and hope would also bear witness to the courage and enduring spirit of the Frank family.

Shadows Over Europe

As the Frank family tried to find peace in their new home in Amsterdam, the geopolitical landscape of Europe was undergoing massive shifts, driven by Adolf Hitler's insatiable appetite for territorial expansion and his ideological campaign. The annexation of Austria in March 1938, known as the Anschluss, marked a significant step in Hitler's plan to unify all German-speaking peoples under the banner of the Third Reich.¹ This move, executed under the disguise of unification, was met with jubilation in some areas but also with

---

1. The term "Third Reich" refers to the state officially known as the German Reich or Nazi Germany, which existed from 1933 to 1945 under the dictatorship of Adolf Hitler and the National Socialist (Nazi) Party. It's called the "Third" Reich because it was considered by the Nazis as the successor to two previous German states. The first was the Holy Roman Empire of the German Nation (considered to have lasted from 962 to 1806), and the second was the German

fear and apprehension in others, as it signaled the beginning of aggressive territorial expansion by Nazi Germany.

The dismemberment of Czechoslovakia further exemplified Hitler's aggressive ambitions. In September 1938, the Munich Agreement permitted Nazi Germany's annexation of the Sudetenland, a region of Czechoslovakia with a significant German-speaking population, under the false excuse of self-determination for ethnic Germans. This was followed by the complete occupation of Czechoslovakia in March 1939, which effectively erased the country from the map of Europe. These actions were not merely territorial conquests but were intrinsically linked to Hitler's broader racial ideology.

Both the Anschluss and the dismemberment of Czechoslovakia were justified through Hitler's distorted racial idea, with claims that the German-speaking populations of these regions were part of the "Aryan master race" and thus rightfully belonged under German rule. By the term "Aryan," Hitler referred to a supposed racial group he considered to be superior and the true foundation of German society. In his distorted view, Aryans were characterized by distinct features such as blonde hair and blue eyes, traits he associated with purity and superiority. This concept was not based on scientific fact but rather on a mixture of pseudo-science, mythology, and racism.

These moves were stark demonstrations of how Hitler's racial policies were entwined with his foreign policy and ambitions for expansion. They served as obvious signs of the extent to which Hitler was willing to go to realize his vision of a racially "pure" Greater German Reich. The aggressive annexation of territories not only threatened the peace of Europe but also directly challenged the existing international order, leading to increased tensions among European powers.

Empire (1871–1918), which ended with the defeat of Germany in World War I and the abdication of Kaiser Wilhelm II.

This period of expansion was a clear manifestation of the dangers posed by the Nazi regime, not only to the sovereignty of nations but also to the very fabric of European society, as it sought to redraw borders based on racial ideologies and the suppression of perceived "inferior" peoples. For Jewish families like the Franks, these developments brought forward the escalating persecution and violence they would face.

Following the annexation of Austria and Czechoslovakia, Hitler's gaze turned toward Poland. The non-aggression pact between Nazi Germany and the Soviet Union in August 1939, known as the Molotov-Ribbentrop Pact, set the stage for the invasion of Poland. On September 1, 1939, Germany invaded Poland, a move that brought about the outbreak of World War II. This invasion demonstrated Hitler's willingness to use military force to achieve his objectives while disregarding international treaties and the sovereignty of nations. The swift and brutal campaign against Poland was not only about territorial gains but also marked the beginning of the racial cleansing that would come to define the Nazi regime.

The concept of Lebensraum, or "living space," was central to Hitler's ideology. He believed that the expansion of German territory was essential for the nation's survival and prosperity. Eastern Europe was chosen as the region to create this space, requiring the control and displacement of the people living there. This policy led to the planned and systematic displacement, enslavement, and extermination of millions of people, particularly Jews, Slavs, Roma, and others deemed "inferior" according to Nazi racial ideology.

Germany's invasion of Poland had catalyzed the outbreak of World War II, as Britain and France declared war on Germany in response. The war quickly spread, engulfing much of Europe. The Netherlands, with its strategic location and attempts to maintain neutrality as it had in World War I, found itself in a risky position. However, the Dutch hope for neutrality was shattered on May 10, 1940, when Germany launched a surprise invasion. The Dutch military, overwhelmed by the superior German forces, gave in after just five days of fighting, marking the beginning of a five-year occupation.

For the Franks and other Jewish families in Amsterdam, the German occupation marked a drastic turn in their fortunes. Initially, life continued with some semblance of normalcy, but it was not long before the Nazi regime began implementing anti-Jewish measures in the Netherlands. Jewish-owned businesses were Aryanized, meaning they were transferred to non-Jewish owners, and Jews were progressively excluded from public life. Otto Frank, in an effort to safeguard his business, transferred ownership to non-Jewish colleagues who were already part of the company's fabric.

Signs reading "Forbidden for Jews" appeared in parks, cinemas, and restaurants, effectively segregating and separating the Jewish population from the rest of society. Jewish individuals were already forbidden from owning cars under the Nazi rule, and the restrictions only intensified when they were subsequently prohibited from riding bicycles. A strict curfew was imposed, commanding that all Jews should be confined to their homes from eight in the evening until six the following morning. This restriction extended to any form of being "outside," including standing on one's balcony or sitting in the backyard. Violation of this curfew, regardless of age, resulted in arrest.

The gradual stripping away of rights from the Jewish people was a methodical and cruel aspect of the Nazi occupation. The occupiers not only deprived Jews of their freedoms but also sought to humiliate them publicly, emphasizing their intent to exclude them from society and degrade them. An obvious illustration of this tactic occurred in the summer of 1941 when the Nazi authorities mandated that Jewish children were to be segregated educationally, attending only Jewish-designated schools. This policy wasn't made public during the summer break; instead, it was enforced at the onset of the new school term. Jewish students, including Anne, were abruptly removed from their classes, a deliberate move designed to isolate them and mark them as outsiders within their own communities.

According to the new regulations imposed by the Nazis, Anne was forbidden from continuing her education at the Montessori School. Instead, she, along with her sister Margot, were required to enroll in the Jewish Lyceum, a secondary school established exclusively for Jewish students in Amsterdam, which opened its doors in September 1941. Despite these adversities, Anne managed to find moments of comfort in the company of friends like Hanne, demonstrating resilience in the face of systemic oppression.

In July 1942, the situation took a more sinister turn with the start of mass deportations. The Jewish population was ordered to report for "work in the East," a euphemism for deportation to concentration and extermination camps. The deliberate targeting of Jews went beyond just stripping them of their economic and social rights. Acts of violence against Jewish individuals became more frequent, peaking in mass arrests and deportations to concentration camps. In one harrowing instance, four hundred Jewish men were seized in broad daylight, most of whom would never return. This act of aggression sparked a rare display of the public's lack of agreement with these policies – a countrywide strike demonstrating the Dutch populace's outrage at the treatment of their Jewish neighbors. However, such acts of solidarity were unable to stop the Nazis' oppressive measures.

Despite the occupation's hardships, life in Amsterdam offered glimpses of resistance and resilience. The occupation of the Netherlands also had profound implications for the Dutch population. The economy was adjusted toward the German war effort, leading to shortages and forced labor. The Dutch resistance movement emerged, conducting acts of sabotage, aiding Jews in hiding, and distributing underground newspapers. However, these acts of defiance were met with brutal repression, including executions and retaliation raids by the German occupiers.

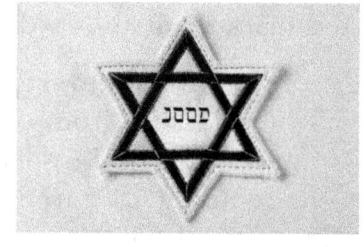

As the war progressed, the Nazi authorities implemented a series of measures aimed at isolating the Jewish population from the rest of society. One of the most visible and infamous of these was the requirement for all Jews to wear identifiers in public, most notably yellow stars. These stars, which were required to be visibly attached to the clothing, bore the word "Jood," the Dutch term for "Jew," making it impossible for Jewish individuals to move through society without instant recognition and discrimination.

This measure was not just about identification; it served to stigmatize and dehumanize Jews, separating them further from non-Jewish communities and making them easy targets for persecution and violence. The imposition of the yellow star was a clear step toward the Nazi goal of total social exclusion of Jewish people, leading to their eventual deportation to concentration and extermination camps. In addition to wearing the yellow star, Jewish families faced increasingly restrictive laws that limited their freedom in almost every aspect of daily life.

Amidst the shadows of occupation and the tightening noose of restrictions placed on Jewish citizens, the Frank family, embodying resilience and a determined spirit, sought and found moments of light and regularity. Their efforts to maintain a semblance of their former life under increasingly dire circumstances were a testament to their strength and ability to find joy in the smallest of pleasures.

The Franks cherished their friendships deeply, relying on these bonds not just for emotional support but also as vital connections to the world outside their immediate circle. These relationships provided an appearance of normalcy and a reminder of the life they once openly lived. Friends offered a lifeline through which the Franks could momentarily forget the direness of their situation, sharing laughter and companionship even as the world outside grew increasingly hostile.

Nature also served as a refuge for the Frank family, especially during brief stays in the countryside during the summers before their life in hiding. These moments, spent in the beauty of the natural world, offered a temporary escape from the oppressive atmosphere of the Nazi-occupied city. The tranquility of the countryside, with its expansive skies, fresh air, and the quiet nature of rural life, provided a stark contrast to the tension and fear that marked their existence in Amsterdam. For Anne and her family, these visits into nature were cherished opportunities to breathe freely, if only for a short while.

Moreover, the celebration of a family friend's wedding offered a rare occasion for genuine joy and celebration. Such events were precious, allowing the Franks and their community to gather, celebrate love and companionship, and momentarily put aside the weight of their circumstances. These celebrations were acts of defiance in their own right, affirming life, hope, and community bonds in the face of systematic dehumanization.

For Anne, in particular, these moments outside the looming shadow of war and persecution were also times of personal growth and exploration. Her visit to a friend's home in the country became a setting for the awakening of adolescent curiosities and interests, notably her budding interest in boys. This aspect of her life highlights the complexity of her experience during the occupation – while living under the constant threat of persecution, she was also navigating the universal challenges and wonders of growing up.

Into Hiding: The Secret Annex

As the Nazis extended their oppressive reach into the Netherlands, the Franks were compelled to make a drastic decision that would separate them from the world outside: going into hiding. This decision was accelerated by the steadily increasing persecution of Jews in Nazi-occupied Amsterdam. The enactment of discriminatory laws, the seizure of businesses, and the ominous deportations signaled a dire need for a place of refuge. Otto Frank, ever wise and foresighted, began preparations for his family's concealment in the annex of his business premises at 263 Prinsengracht. This hidden annex would become a sanctuary of sorts for the Franks and four other individuals seeking solace from the storm of hatred brewing outside.

The meticulous planning involved furnishing the Secret Annex with the necessities of daily life while ensuring it remained invisible to the outside world. Books, clothing, food, and other essentials were smuggled into the annex over time, all under the guise of normal business activities to avoid suspicion. The entrance to their hidden home was concealed behind a movable bookcase, designed to offer no hint of the life behind it. For months, Otto and Edith secretly furnished this hideaway with necessities, ensuring it would be ready when the time came. Their efforts mirrored those of many other Jewish families across the Netherlands, evidence of the desperate measures required for survival during those dark times. This preparation was not only a strategic endeavor but also an emotional one, as the Franks had to make themselves used to the reality of their upcoming lives in isolation.

Otto and Edith Frank had been weighing the heavy decision to vanish into hiding with their daughters to seek refuge from the threatening oppression in Amsterdam. They aimed for a mid-July disappearance, a plan carefully crafted to ensure the safety and continuity of their family unit. However, the course of their carefully laid plans was abruptly altered when, on July 5, a call-up notice for Margot arrived from the Central Office for Jewish Emigration. This notice was not merely a summoning call; rather it was a dire warning, demanding Margot's relocation to a work camp. Like many before, this was a thinly veiled notice of the dark realities of deportation and the unknown horrors that lay beyond. Confronted with the absolute immediacy of this threat, the Frank family's decision crystallized with urgent clarity. The timeline was suddenly compressed, propelling them into hiding ten days sooner than they had intended. This decision was charged with the desperation and determination to escape from the clutches of an increasingly hostile regime.

In the midst of these escalating tensions and the family's frantic preparations for their secret life, Anne Frank celebrated her thirteenth birthday on June 12, 1942. The absence of one cherished figure cast a shadow over the festivities. Her beloved Oma had passed away the previous winter, leaving a void that made the day feel less significant to Anne. Despite this, the Frank family maintained their tradition of celebrating with warmth and joy. This year was marked by a special gathering that included both boys and girls, with Anne's mother preparing a delicious cake and her father showing a film about the adventures of Rin Tin Tin, a brave dog. It was a memorable celebration, rich with the love and care that defined the Frank family's gatherings, yet it was to be the last birthday party Anne would enjoy in the freedom of her pre-hiding life.

On this day, she received a gift that would become an enduring symbol of her voice and legacy: an autograph book, decorated with a red-and-white checkered cloth and secured with a small lock. This book, named 'Kitty' by Anne, was destined for a purpose far beyond the collection of signatures. Anne instilled it with her innermost thoughts, dreams, and observations, transforming it into a diary that would become an emblem of human resilience and insight. Kitty became Anne's confidante, aware of every thought and feeling, from her crushes and quarrels with friends to the books that captured her imagination. Kitty was the silent friend who always listened, never judged. She began writing almost immediately, her initial entries not only chronicling the personal and mundane but also providing a detailed account of the increasing restrictions placed upon the Dutch Jewish community. Notably, Anne wrote her diary in Dutch, although she occasionally incorporated German or English words, reflecting her linguistic versatility. Through her words, Anne painted a vivid picture of a world constricting around her, even as she stood on the threshold of her own hidden journey.

"I hope I will be able to confide everything to you, as I have never been able to confide in anyone, and I hope you will be a great source of comfort and support," Anne mused in her first entry, expressing a profound hope for the diary to be a companion for her innermost thoughts and a pillar of support through the trials that lay ahead. This hope marked the beginning of an intimate dialogue that would extend beyond the personal, shedding light on the grim reality of life under the Nazi persecution.

As the reality of their situation grew more pressing, Anne's transition from the routine of her earlier life to the secrecy of hiding became marked by acts of farewell, symbolized by the parting with her possessions – a poignant reminder of the sacrifices made on the path to preserving their lives. In the days leading up to their disappearance, Anne faced the heart-wrenching task of parting with her possessions. She entrusted her friend and neighbor, Toosje Kupers, with a book, a tea set, and a cherished tin of marbles. Anne expressed her concerns to Toosje, fearing her beloved marbles might end up in the wrong hands, and asked if she could safeguard them.

On the eve of their disappearance, Margot and Anne packed their school bags with essentials, unaware of their destination. Anne included personal items alongside her diary – the plaid cloth-covered book that had become an extension of herself. The family wore multiple layers of clothing to avoid suspicion, leaving behind their home and life as they knew it, with Otto leaving a deceptive note to mislead anyone who might wonder about their abrupt departure. On July 6, leaving behind a note for the Kupers family to care for their cat, Moortje, the Franks stepped into the unknown, leaving their former lives behind to seek refuge in the hidden annex.

Within the concealed world, the Frank family and their fellow hideaways found a semblance of peace and survival through the unwavering support of a small group of Otto Frank's employees. Victor Kugler, Johannes Kleiman, Miep Gies, Bep

Voskuijl, along with Gies' husband, Jan, and Voskuijl's father, Johannes Hendrik, became the lifelines to the outside world for those in hiding. These courageous individuals, aware of the dangers they faced, including the threat of the death penalty for harboring Jews, became the essential link between the hidden and the outside world. They not only kept the annex's occupants informed of war news and political developments but also ensured their sustenance, safety, and morale during the most desperate times. Their dedication to safeguarding the lives of the Franks and their companions emphasized the profound acts of humanity in the middle of a world filled with inhumanity and hatred for the Jews.

The Secret Annex, though a sanctuary, was a place of cramped quarters and constant vigilance. Spanning two small floors and totaling only fifty square yards (approximately 450 square feet or about forty-two square meters), the annex was composed of a few modest rooms. The living space was equipped with a stove, a sink, and a solitary bathroom, while the upper floor contained narrow sleeping quarters for Otto and Edith, and another for Margot and Anne. It was here, in these confined spaces, that Anne found comfort in the familiar, surrounding herself with postcards and photographs of movie stars, including her favorite, Deanna Durbin, and images of royal families, notably Princess Elizabeth and Princess Margaret of England. These mementos, pre-arranged by Otto, transformed the bare walls into a world filled with Anne's interests and aspirations, offered a resemblance of mundane life, and added a personal touch to the family's hidden chamber.

In the attic which was a depository for their food supplies, Anne discovered solitude and a connection to the outside world through the small windows – one offering a view of a tall clock tower, the other of a large chestnut tree. This space became her refuge for reflection, a precious escape within their secluded existence. Their arrival in the annex was a whirlwind of activity, unpacking boxes, and setting up their new living quarters amidst the remnants of their former lives.

To maintain their invisibility, the annex's residents adhered to strict rules: curtains sewn by Anne and her father covered the windows, footsteps were silenced by bare feet and soft slippers, and whispers replaced spoken words. The daily routine was dictated by the necessity to remain undetected by the workers in the building below – no flushing of toilets, no running of water during the hours of business. Every action was calculated, from the burning of trash after dark to the careful management of noise, encapsulating their life in shadows and silence. The importance of remaining undetected during the day meant that the inhabitants had to be exceedingly quiet, a rule that led to its own set of challenges. Anne recounted instances of accidental noises that sparked fear and tension among the group, such as dropping a utensil or moving too loudly, each sound a reminder of the constant danger they faced.

The annex's population soon grew, as the Van Pels family – Mr. and Mrs. Van Pels and their son, Peter, accompanied by Peter's cat, Mouschi – joined the Franks. The arrival of these new companions added complexity to the dynamics within the annex but also brought additional warmth and solidarity to their secluded community. Together, they navigated the challenges and intricacies of hidden life, bound by the common hope for freedom and the relentless pursuit of survival under the watchful care of their dedicated helpers.

The Annex: A Microcosm of Hope and Resilience

In July of 1942, the dynamic within the Secret Annex had already begun to evolve with the arrival of the Van Pels family: Hermann, Auguste, and their 16-year-old son, Peter. Later the dynamic changed further with the arrival of Fritz Pfeffer, a dentist and acquaintance of the Franks, in November. Anne initially welcomed the arrival of new faces into their secluded world as she was eager for the fresh conversations and perspectives they promised. However, the changes required to host the additional company soon gave way to the strains and stresses of communal living under such restrictive conditions. Life in the Annex, though shielded from the direct horrors of the war, was far from easy. The crowded conditions led to inevitable quarrels among its inhabitants, with Anne often finding herself at the center of disputes.

Anne's relationship with Fritz Pfeffer became particularly strained after they began sharing a room. She found him intolerable, struggling with his presence in what was once her personal space. She was particularly annoyed by his insistence on strict adherence to room-sharing schedules and his use of their shared space, which often disregarded her privacy and study time. Similarly, her interactions with Auguste van Pels were fraught with tension; Anne viewed her as lacking in sense. Anne's views on Auguste van Pels were mixed but leaned toward the negative due to Auguste's behaviors that Anne perceived as vain and overly concerned with appearances. Auguste's attitudes toward the food and her dramatic reactions to the hardships of life in hiding often led to conflicts and tension within the Annex. Anne observed these behaviors with a critical eye, taking note of the strain they put on communal living. Her opinions of Hermann van Pels and Fritz Pfeffer leaned toward viewing them as selfish, especially concerning their food consumption, which, in the context of their limited resources, became a significant point of disagreement.

Despite these challenges with the others, Anne's relationship with Peter van Pels underwent a remarkable transformation. Initially, she was dismissive of Peter, finding him shy and awkward which she wrote about as, "For the rest, things are going better. I don't think Peter's gotten any nicer. He's an obnoxious boy who lies around on his bed all day, only rousing himself to do a little carpentry work before returning to his nap. What a dope!" Over time, however, she discovered a sense of kinship with him, and the two developed a romantic connection. Anne's diary recounts the thrill of receiving her first kiss from Peter, a moment of intimacy and connection in the middle of their isolation. Reflecting on this budding relationship with Peter, Anne mused, "But seriously, I don't think it's at all shocking; we're cooped up here, cut off from the world, anxious and fearful, especially lately. Why should we stay apart when we love each other? Why shouldn't we kiss each other in times like these? Why should we wait until we've reached a suitable age? Why should we ask anybody's permission?" This candid introspection by Anne depicted a bigger universal theme: the natural human longing for closeness and understanding, especially in times of adversity. Yet, as their relationship progressed, Anne began to question the depth of her feelings for him, pondering whether they were a true reflection of her heart or a product of their shared circumstances. Her questioning underlines a mature introspection about love, companionship, and the essence of genuine connection during the most trying times.

In the middle of the complexities of these relationships within the Annex, Anne formed particularly close bonds with the group of helpers who facilitated their life in hiding. Her anticipation for their daily visits was a highlight of her existence in confinement, a connection to the outside world that brought her immense joy and comfort. Anne Frank's relationship with Bep Voskuijl is notably warm and caring, as evidenced by Anne's detailed account of Bep's engagement in her diary entry dated Thursday, May 25, 1944. Anne reveals a deep concern for Bep's happiness and future, expressing reservations about Bep's engagement to Bertus, a young man whom Anne believes Bep does not truly love. She describes Bertus as a steady but unambitious laborer, suggesting that Bep is settling for security rather than genuine affection. Anne's reflection on Bep's reasons for the engagement – pressure from her family, concerns about being an "old maid," and her father's fondness for Bertus – shows Anne's understanding and empathy for Bep's situation. Despite her concerns, Anne hoped for the best for Bep, wishing her happiness and that Bertus might improve under Bep's influence or that she might find someone more compatible.

This detailed observation of Bep's personal life, coupled with Anne's expressed desire for Bep's happiness, emphasizes the closeness of their relationship. Anne's willingness to delve into the complexities of Bep's emotional life, and her candid expression of hope and concern for her friend, underscore the special bond they shared. This friendship offered Anne a source of strength and connection beyond the immediate circle of her family and fellow annex residents while providing a lifeline to the outside world and a reminder of the normalcy and personal concerns that persisted even in the face of the war's chaos and horror.

The routine of the Annex was punctuated by the pursuit of education and the attempt to maintain a semblance of routine. Otto Frank took on the role of teacher, guiding his daughters and Peter through their studies.  Anne's disdain for math was matched only by her determination to keep up with her academic aspirations as her intellectual curiosity kept undimmed by the confines of their hideout. Anne and the others found a special kind of freedom through their love for books, learning, and creativity. Writing in her diary became Anne's way to explore her thoughts and dreams, almost like a key unlocking a door to a wider world beyond the Annex's walls. They all shared books and enjoyed lively discussions that brought a bit of normal life into their hidden existence. This was not just a way to pass the time; it was how they kept their spirits up and remembered who they were – vibrant, curious individuals, not just people hiding away. Anne's growing passion for writing, her and the others' dedication to learning new languages, and their deep dives into literature were acts of resistance, proving that their spirits couldn't be caged by the walls around them.

As the days turned into months within the confines of the Secret Annex, the challenges faced by its inhabitants grew increasingly dire. Food became scarcer, and the shadow of discovery loomed large, threatening their fragile existence at every moment. Anne noted several occasions where the distribution and preparation of food led to disputes, underscoring the stress of rationing scarce resources. An instance involved the disagreement over the division of butter, reflecting broader tensions over equal sharing of resources. Mrs. van Daan's particular habits, such as hoarding food for her son, Peter, and the complaint about Anne's liberal use of sugar for her jam, illustrate the ongoing negotiation and compromise required in their communal living situation.

Living in such close quarters meant that personal habits and hygiene practices, which in ordinary circumstances would be private matters, became sources of communal concern and, at times, conflict. Anne humorously mentioned the use of Mrs. van Daan's chamber pot, a private item made communal, as a symbol of the blurred lines between personal and shared spaces. Additionally, the allocation of scarce resources like water for bathing was a logistical challenge that required careful planning and negotiation.

Beyond the practical challenges, the emotional and psychological toll of living in hiding was significant. Anne detailed the fluctuations in mood among the inhabitants from bouts of depression to moments of irritability; all the emotions were amplified by their confinement. The stress of their situation sometimes led to outbursts over trivial matters, serving as outlets for deeper, unspoken anxieties. The intensity of the Annex's environment magnified personal differences and led to conflicts, such as the one between Anne and Mrs. van Daan over Anne's maturity and behavior.

Among these challenges and the oppressive silence necessitated by their risky situation, an incident that showcased their vulnerability occurred one seemingly ordinary morning. Peter, upon going down to the warehouse, was met with a sight that sent a ripple of alarm through the hidden residents: both the warehouse and street doors stood open. This breach of their sanctuary's security led to an immediate and practiced response among the residents. The household fell into a silent state, adhering to the strict protocol designed to hide any indication of their presence. This incident, while it did not have any direct confrontation, served as a dark reminder of the ever-present threat lurking just beyond their walls, casting a shadow over their already strained existence.

The discovery that burglars had come as far as the office below them, stealing things yet missing the secret above, seemed like a narrow escape. Anne detailed the incident with a sense of foreboding, "He told that the burglars had forced the outside door and the warehouse door with a crowbar, but when they didn't find anything worth stealing, they tried their luck on the next floor. They stole two cash boxes containing 40 guilders(equivalent to 714 USD in today's currency), blank checkbooks and, worst of all, coupons for 330 pounds of sugar, our entire allotment. It won't be easy to wangle new ones." This episode brought more than the worry of physical loss. It was the stark realization of the threat such incidents posed to their already fragile semblance of stability. The challenge of replacing these essential goods underscored the continuous effort required to sustain their hidden existence, deepening the sense of isolation and vulnerability that pervaded the Annex.

Amidst this atmosphere of constant uncertainty and deprivation, Anne Frank found solace and strength in the pages of her diary. Her entries, once focused on the day-to-day, deepened into thoughtful meditations on the nature of war and her longing for peace. Through her words, Anne's intellectual and physical growth shone as a beacon of resilience, demonstrating the unwavering strength of the human spirit even in the darkest times. Despite the daily challenges, moments of lightheartedness and warmth also came into the Annex. Anne's infatuation with the movies and her collection of postcards and photographs provided a welcome escape from the grim realities of their situation. The bond between the helpers and those in hiding deepened, with Miep Gies and her husband, Jan, spending a night in the

Annex, offering Gies and her husband a poignant insight into the constant fear that defined Anne and the others' existence.

In this secluded world, the role of the helpers also became increasingly vital. Miep Gies was often the first to arrive in the morning while the office was still quiet and she would collect the day's shopping list from Edith Frank or Mrs. Van Pels. She navigated the dangerous streets of Amsterdam, where carrying too much food could arouse suspicion, to bring back necessities. Miep also smuggled in a stream of books and newspapers, keeping the hidden group connected to the outside world. Her visits were not just about bringing physical sustenance but also news of friends and events outside, which Anne eagerly awaited.

Bep Voskuijl, the young typist, played a crucial role in maintaining the secrecy of the Annex. She helped manage the office affairs to ensure that the hidden floor's existence remained undiscovered. An anecdote that illustrates her dedication involved Bep crafting false ration cards to procure the extra food necessary to sustain the eight hidden lives, a risky endeavor that could have led to her arrest.

Victor Kugler, often referred to by Anne as "Mr. Kraler," took on the perilous task of arranging for the delivery of food supplies and other essentials. One particular story of his bravery involved Victor cycling through the countryside to acquire black market food when supplies in the city became too risky to obtain. On the other hand, Johannes Kleiman's role involved more administrative and logistical support, ensuring that the business continued to operate smoothly as a cover for the Annex. He handled the complex task of managing the company's affairs in such a way that attention was never drawn to the hidden inhabitants upstairs. Johannes was also involved in arranging for secret messages to be sent to family members of those in hiding, providing a precious line of communication with the outside world.

The profound acts of courage displayed by the helpers, in both significant and subtle ways, transcended mere physical support for those hidden within the Secret Annex. Their efforts represented a bold stance against the tyranny of the Nazis, with each act of assistance serving as a defiance to the regime's oppressive forces. The influx of external information, stealthily provided by these brave souls, was a lifeline for the Annex's residents, tying them to the outside world from which they were cut off. Radios smuggled in by the helpers became crucial channels, not only for news but as symbols of hope, connecting the hidden group to the global struggle unfolding beyond their concealed walls.

This connection was especially felt on June 6, 1944, a day marked by the Allied forces' invasion of Normandy, an event that became known as D-Day. Far from being a distant military maneuver, the invasion gave a flicker of hope for the Annex's inhabitants. Anne captured the essence of this monumental day in her diary with visible excitement and a detailed account of the unfolding events. She wrote, "This is the day. The invasion has begun!" Anne detailed the heavy bombings reported by the British at strategic locations and the consequent warnings issued to those living near the coast. Her recounting of the BBC broadcasts throughout the day, including speeches by notable leaders and the confirmation that "This is 0 Day" reflected not just a historical account but a personal testament to the hope ignited within the confines of their hiding place.

Anne's reflection, "Oh, Kitty, the best part about the invasion is that I have the feeling that friends are on the way" poignantly expressed the emotional significance of D-Day to those sheltered in the Annex. She spoke of the oppression they had endured and the longing for salvation, emphasizing that the invasion symbolized much more than a military operation; it represented the approach of liberation, not just for the Jews but for all of occupied Europe. The anticipation of returning to a normal life, perhaps even going back to school by fall, underscored the resurgence of hope and the possibility of a future free from tyranny.

This moment, recorded with keen insight by Anne, underscored the deep impact of world events on the small, secluded group, for whom each piece of news was a thread woven into their continued struggle for survival and hope for a future of freedom. The D-Day operation emerged not merely as a strategic battle in the war but as a signal to those hidden in the Annex that the tides might be turning in their favor, hinting at the liberation that lay ahead. Through Anne's eyes, the events of June 6, 1944, were transformed from mere military updates into a ray of hope that penetrated the darkness of their hidden world, illuminating the enduring human spirit's capacity for hope amidst despair.

Another significant event that impacted the mood within the Annex was the liberation of Paris in August 1944. The news of Paris' freedom after years of German occupation brought a wave of optimism to the hidden group, stirring dreams of a return to normalcy and freedom. The joy and relief that Anne described in her diary upon hearing of Paris' liberation reflected the profound emotional connection they all felt to the broader struggle against tyranny.

However, not all news brought hope. The Eastern Front, referring to the conflict between Germany and the Soviet Union, saw some of the war's most brutal fighting and significant shifts in momentum. Reports of the worsening situation there, coupled with the atrocities being uncovered as the Allies advanced, painted a grim picture of the conflict's human cost. Additionally, the bombing of Dutch cities by Allied forces, aimed at undermining German occupation but resulting in civilian casualties and destruction, introduced complex feelings of fear and sorrow. While these actions were part of the broader strategy for liberation, they also underscored the war's tragic toll on innocent lives and the landscapes that once formed the backdrop of daily existence for the people of the Netherlands. Anne's reflections on these events in her diary reveal complex emotions: fear for the safety of those outside, sorrow for the suffering of innocents caught in the crossfire, and the moral quandary posed by the destruction necessary for liberation.

Throughout these turbulent times, the radio broadcasts listened to in secret became nightly rituals, around which the Annex's residents gathered in silence, hanging on every word. The voices from the radio brought the war into their hidden chamber, making it a tangible presence that shaped their daily existence. These broadcasts, and the discussions that followed, served not only as a source of news but as a forum for education, debate, and the strengthening of their communal bonds. In chronicling these events and their impact, Anne's diary serves as a poignant window into how the macrocosm of war penetrated the microcosm of the Secret Annex.

Later, Otto Frank reflected on the significance of these relationships and time for Anne, noting her impatient enthusiasm for the helpers' visits and the particular closeness she felt with Bep. These connections, both within the tight-knit group of the Annex and with their external lifelines, underscored the human capacity for resilience, friendship, and hope amidst the direst circumstances.

Anne's World Within Walls

Gifted with a diary on her thirteenth birthday, Anne embarked on a written journey that would transcend the confines of her hidden world. The act of writing offered Anne not just solace but also a sense of freedom. Through her words, she crafted a bridge from the isolation of the Annex to the vast, tumultuous world outside. She wrote with a poignancy and wisdom far beyond her years, reflecting on the nature of humanity, the cruelty of persecution, and the irrationality of war. Yet, interwoven with these reflections were the everyday concerns and joys of adolescence – the flutter of first love, the friction with family members, the cherished friendships, and the longing for independence. The dynamics of her family, the evolving bond with Peter van Pels, and the interactions with the other inhabitants offered a miniature image of society, a stage on which the dramas of human interaction unfolded.

Through these relationships, Anne explored themes of love, conflict, companionship, and forgiveness, reflecting on the ways in which human connections can both challenge and sustain us.

Anne Frank embarked on an introspective journey, dissecting the intricate web of her family relationships through the lens of her diary. Central to this exploration was her relationship with her father, Otto Frank, who stood as her emotional anchor and the person with whom Anne felt the deepest connection. This profound bond was captured in Anne's own words, "Daddy's a sweetheart; he may get mad at me, but it never lasts longer than five minutes." Anne's relationship with her father, Otto Frank, indeed stood as a cornerstone of her emotional and psychological sustenance during their time in hiding. While she shared a profound connection with him, exemplified by affection and mutual respect, instances of tension and misunderstanding did emerge, depicting the complexities of their bond under the strains of their secluded life.

One poignant example of strain in their relationship occurred when Anne, in a moment of profound self-reflection and regret, acknowledged the unjust harshness of her words toward her father. She admitted to having failed miserably in accusing her father, whom she referred to as "Pim," of not understanding her. With a heart of gold, she described this as the worst thing she had ever done. This episode is emblematic of the occasional rifts that could surface in their relationship, stemming from Anne's rapidly growing self-awareness and her struggle with the confines of their shared existence.

Despite such moments of tension, Anne's deep affection and respect for her father consistently shine through her writings. She often regarded him as her moral compass and emotional anchor, even as she grappled with the normal developmental push for autonomy and identity formation which are characteristics of adolescence. For instance, Anne's struggle with her identity and place within her family is evident when she discusses feeling neglected and misunderstood, not only by her mother but also, to a lesser extent, by her father. She wished for her father to see her as Anne, her own person, rather than just his child.

Moreover, Anne's introspective journey within the confines of the Annex led her to a sophisticated understanding of her own need for privacy and independence. This understanding sometimes put her at odds with her father's protective and parental instincts, as she sought to navigate her own path toward maturity and self-reliance. Her reflective process about her relationship with her father, coupled with her acute self-awareness, underscores the evolving nature of their bond.

Reflecting on their relationship, Otto Frank later mused that his bond with Anne was stronger, possibly because Margot, her sister, was more reserved and self-sufficient and gravitated toward their mother and didn't seek the same level of emotional support that Anne did. This dynamic within the Frank family illustrates the individual relationships that shaped Anne's world, with her father's guidance and love providing a foundation of security and encouragement in the tumultuous landscape of their lives in hiding.

Anne's relationship with her sister Margot evolved significantly during their time in hiding. Initially, Anne viewed Margot through the lens of sibling rivalry, feeling that Margot was the favored child, praised for her calm demeanor and intellectual abilities. However, Anne's perceptions and feelings toward Margot underwent profound changes as their circumstances demanded a deeper connection beyond typical sibling interactions.

One incident described in Anne's diary involved a dispute over a book, reflecting the typical tensions of sharing limited resources and space. Margot had been reading a book and set it aside; when Anne picked it up to look at the pictures, Margot demanded it back, leading to a conflict that involved their parents taking Margot's side. Anne expressed frustration not just with the outcome but with the perceived injustice of the situation and her parents' intervention on Margot's behalf. She felt a deep injustice at being scolded without a fair hearing, a sentiment that extended to her broader feelings of being misunderstood and marginalized within her family dynamics, particularly compared to Margot.

Despite these moments of tension and competition, Anne's diary also reveals her growing admiration and affection for Margot. Anne acknowledged Margot's virtues and her own evolving feelings, moving from jealousy to a recognition of Margot's intrinsic qualities of goodness and understanding. This change in perspective is focused on in Anne's writings, where she stated she never felt jealous of Margot, making it clear that her envy was not about Margot's smarts or looks. Instead, Anne desired acknowledgment for her unique self from their father, whom she deeply adored.

Margot Frank's character, often described through Anne's perspective, reveals a deep level of emotional intelligence and maturity. The event regarding Anne's relationship with Peter van Daan serves as a significant example of Margot's inherent selflessness and her capacity for empathy, even in the face of personal loneliness.

Margot's response to Anne's growing closeness with Peter was marked by a profound understanding and acceptance, rare for someone of her age and in their circumstances. In a period marked by confinement and constant proximity, where personal space and privacy were virtually nonexistent, emotions could easily have been heightened, leading to jealousy and conflict. However, Margot chose a path of understanding and support.

The context of Margot's reaction is rooted in the unique pressures of their life in hiding. The Annex provided limited opportunities for personal growth and social interactions, especially with peers. For Margot and Anne, the arrival of the van Pels family, including Peter, introduced a new dynamic to their secluded world. Anne's subsequent bond with Peter could have been a source of dispute between the sisters, given the scarcity of companionship.

However, Margot's letter to Anne, where she openly discussed her feelings, is evidence for her introspective nature and her desire to see Anne happy. Margot recognized the importance of the friendship between Anne and Peter, not just for its emotional support but also as a critical element of their survival strategy in the oppressive environment of the Annex. By encouraging Anne to value and nurture her relationship with Peter, Margot demonstrated a level of self-awareness and altruism that went beyond typical sibling interactions.

This act of encouragement and reassurance from Margot not only showcases her capacity for empathy but also underscores the evolving nature of her relationship with Anne. As Anne navigated her feelings for Peter, Margot's support provided a foundation of trust and understanding, deepening the bond between the sisters. Margot's ability to put Anne's emotional needs above her own illustrates her empathy and kindness, qualities that Anne grew to recognize and appreciate deeply.

Through these anecdotes, Anne Frank's diary offers a window into the complexities of her relationship with Margot, marked by the normalcy of sibling rivalry yet profoundly shaped by the extraordinary circumstances of their life in hiding. The evolution of Anne's feelings toward Margot, from rivalry to deep affection and respect, mirrors Anne's own journey of self-discovery and maturation.

Similarly, Anne's relationship with her mother, Edith Frank, was one of the most complex and evolving aspects of her diary. Initially, Anne expressed significant frustration and criticism

 toward her mother, feeling misunderstood and unfairly treated. However, over time, Anne's reflections show a journey toward understanding and introspection, revealing her growth and maturity amidst the challenging conditions of their hiding.

Anne openly discussed her struggles with her mother, admitting to feelings of anger and frustration. In an entry dated Thursday, January 6, 1944, Anne candidly shared her realizations about their relationship, acknowledging her part in their strained interactions: "I was furious at Mother (and still am a lot of time)... It's true she didn't understand me, but I didn't understand her either." This moment of introspection marked a turning point for Anne, as she began to see the complexities of their relationship from a more mature perspective.

Anne's changing view of her mother is also shown in a touching diary entry where her mother tries to bond with her by offering to hear her prayers, but Anne turns her down. Reflecting on her harsh response, Anne recognized her mother's pain and expressed remorse for her coldness, revealing a deep empathy and understanding that was developing within her: "Mother got up, stood beside my bed for a moment, and then slowly walked toward the door. Suddenly she turned, her face contorted with pain, and said, 'I don't want to be angry with you. I can't make you love me!'" (Monday, May 8, 1944). This incident sheds light on Anne's growing awareness of her actions' impact on others, especially her mother.

Despite these moments of insight and regret, Anne continued to grapple with conflicting feelings toward her mother. She acknowledged the deep divide between them, feeling that her mother could not truly understand or fulfill her needs as a daughter. Anne's critique was not only of her mother's behavior but also of what she perceived as a lack of maternal instinct: "I need my mother to set a good example and be a person I can respect but in most matters, she's an example of what not to do" (Thursday, January 6, 1944). This sentiment underscored the profound longing Anne felt for a more traditional maternal figure, one who could guide and support her through her formative years.

Anne Frank's reflections on her relationship with her mother provide a nuanced understanding of the complexities inherent in their bond. Through her diary, Anne offered an honest and often critical view of her mother, yet her entries also demonstrate a deep yearning for connection and understanding. As Anne navigated the trials of adolescence in the seclusion of the Annex, her writings reveal a journey toward empathy, maturity, and, ultimately, a form of reconciliation with the imperfections of her familial relationships.

Furthermore, education remained a source of hope for the Frank sisters, a tether to a world and future beyond the Annex. Margot pursued Latin with diligence, achieving high marks in her correspondence courses, while Anne devoted herself to reading, writing, and refining her diary entries. These pursuits were not merely academic; they were acts of defiance against the constraints of their hiding, with Anne's diary serving as both witness and testament to her evolving thoughts, beliefs, and aspirations. Anne's ambition to become a journalist or a writer flourished in the seclusion of the Annex, she wrote in her diary on Wednesday, April 5, 1944:

"I finally realized that I must do my schoolwork to keep from being ignorant, to get on in life, to become a journalist, because that's what I want! I know I can write ..., but it remains to be seen whether I really have talent ...

And if I don't have the talent to write books or newspaper articles, I can always write for myself. But I want to achieve more than that. I can't imagine living like Mother, Mrs. van Daan and all the women who go about their work and are then forgotten. I need to have something besides a husband and children to devote myself to! ...

I want to be useful or bring enjoyment to all people, even those I've never met. I want to go on living even after my death! And that's why I'm so grateful to God for having given me this gift, which I can use to develop myself and to express all that's inside me!

When I write I can shake off all my cares. My sorrow disappears, my spirits are revived! But, and that's a big question, will I ever be able to write something great, will I ever become a journalist or a writer?"

Anne's commitment to her diary remained steadfast, marking her days with the regularity of a heartbeat until her final entry on August 1, 1944. In this entry, she continued her musings from her last entry about contradictions, writing, "A bundle of contradictions' was the end of my previous letter and is the beginning of this one. Can you please tell me exactly what 'a bundle of contradictions' is? What does 'contradiction' mean? Like so many words, it can be interpreted in two ways: a contradiction imposed from without and one imposed from within. The former means not accepting other people's opinions, always knowing best, having the last word; in short, all those unpleasant traits for which I'm known. The latter, for which I'm not known, is my own secret." This discipline of writing became a silent witness to the world she inhabited and thus became an integral part of her daily existence, reflecting her journey of self-discovery and her burgeoning voice as a writer.

Anne's diary entries transformed from mere accounts of daily life into profound reflections on her dreams, the essence of human nature, and her faith. Writing became her solace, a means to transcend the immediate confines of her world and to articulate a vision for her life beyond the war. She aspired not only to remember and be remembered but to leave an unerasable mark on the world through her words. This ambition, coupled with her growing confidence in her talent, underscored her determination to forge a path of significance, far removed from the traditional roles she observed around her.

We're half way there: A note from Scott Matthews

As we find ourselves at the midpoint of the book, delving deeper into the profound journey of Anne Frank's story, I want to express my sincere gratitude to you. The crafting of this narrative has been a labor of empathy, fueled by a profound reverence for Anne's resilience and a commitment to sharing her story with you.

Your engagement and reflections are invaluable not only to me but also to those who seek to comprehend the significance of Anne Frank's legacy. Your reviews not only support my endeavor as a storyteller but also contribute to the collective remembrance of Anne's life. I take to heart each review, treasuring your perspectives and suggestions for further exploration.

If you have found resonance in the pages thus far or have ideas on how we can navigate the remainder of Anne's journey together, I encourage you to take a moment to share your thoughts. A QR code is provided below for your convenience. Whether you are reading digitally or holding a physical copy, a simple scan or click allows you to contribute your reflections.

Thank you for joining in this odyssey. Your feedback not only shapes the narrative but also honors Anne Frank's enduring spirit. Here's to the unfolding chapters and the profound lessons they hold.

Betrayal and Capture

In the tranquility of an Amsterdam morning on August 4, 1944, the sanctuary of the Secret Annex was breached beyond repair. German Security Police, led by an anonymous tip-off, descended upon their refuge. The police was led by SS[1]-Oberscharführer Karl Silberbauer of the Sicherheitsdienst, the

---

1. The SS, or Schutzstaffel, was a major paramilitary organization under Adolf Hitler and the Nazi Party in Nazi Germany. Founded in 1925, it initially served as Hitler's personal bodyguard unit but rapidly expanded in size and scope to become one of the most powerful and feared organizations in the Third Reich. By the start of World War II, the SS had assumed a leading role in the security, surveillance, and extermination operations against Jews, political dissidents, and others deemed as enemies of the state. The SS was responsible for the administration of concentration camps and extermination camps, playing a central role in the Holocaust, where six million Jews were murdered, along with millions of others including Poles, Soviet prisoners of war, Romani people, and people with disabilities.

intelligence agency of the SS and the Nazi Party, in which Silberbauer held the rank of Oberscharführer, which is equivalent to a senior squad leader. This breach marked the end of over two years of hiding for the Frank family, the Van Pelses, and Fritz Pfeffer.

Victor Kugler, who was confronted first by the invaders, attempted to deflect their inquiries. However, Silberbauer's insistence on identifying the person in charge and his order for Kugler to take them upstairs highlighted how serious the situation was. Despite Kugler's initial resistance, the insistence from the Dutch officers (Gezinus Gringhuis, Willem Grootendorst, and possibly Maarten Kuiper) revealed that the secret of the Annex had been compromised. The ensuing arrest was a whirlpool of confusion and despair, abruptly ending the occupants' risky but cherished semblance of safety.

The habitants of the Annex were swiftly taken to the RSHA (Reich Security Main Office) headquarters where they endured a night of interrogation. This was only a prelude to the even harsher conditions they would soon face. The following day, their journey into the unknown began with a transfer to the overcrowded House of Detention of the Weteringschans, a stark contrast to the life they had known in the hidden confines of the Annex. The Annex, once a fortification of hope and resilience, became the setting for their capture, intertwining their fates with the millions captured by the Nazi regime's merciless campaign.

Following their arrest, the group was escorted to the Gestapo (the official secret police of Nazi Germany and in German-occupied Europe) headquarters in Amsterdam. The initial shock of capture gave way to a grim reality as they faced interrogation and detention. Just two days later, a bleak procession to the Westerbork transit camp started, where they were designated as criminals for their act of hiding and subjected to hard labor in the Punishment Barracks. This camp, a somber witness to the tragedy that engulfed over 100,000 Jews from the Netherlands and Germany, stood as a stark testament to the catastrophic events unfolding across Europe.

Meanwhile, Victor Kugler and Johannes Kleiman found themselves captured by the same raid, landing in the penal camp for enemies of the regime at Amersfoort. The penal camp for enemies of the regime was a detention center established by the occupying forces, designed to imprison and punish those who opposed the Nazi regime, including resistance fighters, political protesters, and others deemed a threat to their control. While Kleiman found his release after seven weeks, Kugler faced a more prolonged ordeal, shuffling between various concentration and prison camps until the war's eventual conclusion.

Miep Gies, confronted and threatened by the Security Police, narrowly avoided detention, an example of her courage and the risks she bore. Bep Voskuijl, quick-thinking, managed to salvage crucial documents, preventing further incrimination of those involved in procuring food from the black market. In the days that followed, the two women ventured back into the now-empty Achterhuis, where they discovered Anne's papers scattered and abandoned. With a resolve born of hope, Gies gathered these papers, along with family photo albums, vowing to return them to Anne after the war.

In a poignant act of desperation on August 7, 1944, Gies sought to negotiate the release of the captured group by approaching Silberbauer with an offer of money. Despite her efforts, Silberbauer refused, a stark reminder of the implacability of their captors and the limits of individual action against such overwhelming forces.

Westerbork was like a dark introduction to even harder times that were coming. The infrastructure of Westerbork, designed as a transit camp, operated under a rigorous and unforgiving schedule, a testament to the bureaucratic efficiency that marked the Holocaust's darkest chapters. Each week, typically on Tuesdays, trains departed Westerbork as part of a harsh routine orchestrated by Adolf Eichmann's office, which determined the schedules, destinations, and passenger quotas for these transports. Within the confines of the camp, the responsibility assigned to the Jewish council involved a profoundly distressing task: they were required to compile lists and select individuals for deportation. Each week, on the eve of departure, the names of those chosen for transport were announced, casting a deep and pervasive sense of dread throughout the camp. This grim routine not only showcased the council's agonizing role but also served as a weekly reminder of the camp's dire purpose as a stopping point in the machinery of the Holocaust. This process, marked by its methodical precision, laid bare the chilling efficiency with which lives were uprooted and destinies forever altered.

Even as the dark cloud of future deportations loomed overhead, a fragile sense of normality managed to persist among the prisoners. This delicate balance was maintained through a combination of hope and denial. The prisoners worked under the hopeful assumption that proving themselves indispensable might somehow spare them from being chosen for transport. In an environment defined by fear and uncertainty, they clung to their daily routines and the remnants of their past lives as if they were lifelines, serving as a semblance of normalcy amidst the turmoil. A particularly moving example of this desperate search for normality can be seen in Franz Ledermann's request to have his newspaper redirected to Westerbork. This request was more than just a wish for news from the outside world. It symbolized a profound yearning for any semblance of connection to life beyond the camp's boundaries.

In the Westerbork camp, the rhythm of daily life was starkly interrupted by the regularity of weekly deportations. Despite this, the resilience of the human spirit shone through as the inmates strove to uphold their dignity and foster a sense of community within the confines of their harsh reality. Children and young people were organized into groups to continue their education, an effort to provide a semblance of normalcy to their fraught lives. This continued schooling served as a way to uphold any sense of routine in an environment where the constant departure of peers on transports was a stark reminder of their circumstances. Within this setting, the act of issuing report cards to children before their deportations emerged as a symbol of hope and defiance against the dire future that awaited many of them. These report cards represented more than just an assessment of academic achievement; they were an emblem of the enduring belief in the possibility of a future beyond the camp's barbed wires – a future that, tragically, many of these children would never have the chance to explore.

Anne Frank's experience in Westerbork reflected a spectrum of human emotion, from the degradation of processing and the discomfort of ill-fitting prison clothes to the camaraderie found in shared labor. Tasked with dismantling batteries, a task both boring and hazardous, Anne and her companions sought solace in each other's company, sharing stories and dreams of post-war life.

Edith Frank, in this setting, revealed a previously unseen side of her personality, engaging in heartfelt conversations with fellow prisoners, a reminder of the deep bonds formed in the world of shared suffering. Anne, herself, radiated a combination of youthful vigor and a profound sense of understanding, her behavior reflecting the depth of maturity gained from her hardships and experiences. Despite the difficulties she faced, Anne, along with her fellow prisoners, was driven by the dream of a life beyond the barriers of the camp – a life abundant with freedom and opportunities. This aspiration served as a powerful symbol of the human spirit's unwavering capacity to withstand and maintain hope in the most dire of situations.

The transition from Westerbork to Auschwitz, the notorious Nazi concentration and extermination camp, represented a dark descent into the Holocaust's abyss. On September 3, 1944, crammed into cattle cars devoid of humanity, the Franks embarked on a journey emblematic of the era's atrocities. Among the passengers was Bloeme Evers-Emden, a friend of Margot and Anne from their days at the Jewish Lyceum, who would later recall seeing the Frank family in Auschwitz and share her memories in documentaries, offering a glimpse into their lives during this unimaginable time. The difficult and arduous trek was marked by deprivation and despair, and it ended at the gates of Auschwitz, a place synonymous with the extremes of human cruelty. Eventually, all eight individuals who had found refuge in the Annex found themselves transported to a concentration camp in Poland. There, they were segregated by gender – Mr. Pfeffer, Mr. Van Pels, Peter, and Otto were placed among the men, while Anne, Margot, Edith, and Mrs. Van Pels were sent to the section designated for women. This separation of families upon arrival, with Otto Frank torn from his wife and daughters, underlined the evil and distraught inflicted by the camp's systematic dehumanization.

The brutal selection process then ensued, determining who would be forced into labor and who would face immediate execution. Tragically, of the 1,019 passengers on their transport, 549, including all children under 15, were sent directly to the gas chambers. Anne, having just turned 15, narrowly escaped this fate and was one of the youngest persons to do so.

The women admitted into the camp underwent dehumanizing procedures: they were stripped naked, shaved, disinfected, and tattooed with numbers for identification. Anne, along with the other women, was subjected to grueling slave labor by day and endured overcrowded barracks by night.

Within Auschwitz's confines, the women of the Annex confronted the stark reality of their new existence. Stripped of their identities and subjected to the camp's brutal regime, they grappled with the daily struggle for survival against the backdrop of ever-present mortality. Yet, even in the shadow of such adversity, moments of connection and shared hope persisted, fragile threads of humanity that withstood the surrounding desolation.

Disease ran uncontrolled through the camp, and Anne soon suffered from a severe scabies infection. The Frank sisters were moved to an infirmary, a place plagued by darkness and overrun with bugs and insects. In a heartbreaking act of maternal sacrifice, Edith Frank chose to stop eating, saving her food for her daughters.

As Soviet forces closed in, triggering the SS's decision to evacuate Auschwitz, Anne Frank and her companions faced yet another upheaval. The women of the Frank family were designated for transfer to the Liebau labor camp in October 1944, a move that was also planned for Bloeme Evers-Emden. However, Anne's affliction with scabies meant that she, along with her mother and sister, were forced to remain behind, diverging their journey from that of Bloeme. This separation was not a matter of choice but a stark reflection of the circumstances imposed upon them. It stressed the strong familial bonds and unwavering resolve of the Frank family, who remained united in spirit even as external forces subjected them to continuous hardship.

The capture of the Frank family and the initial days of their incarceration reflect not just on the abrupt end to their life in hiding but also on the resilience, courage, and fleeting moments of hope that defined their existence. The determination of those outside the Annex to safeguard the memory and voice of Anne, symbolized by the preservation of her diary, underscores a profound act of resistance and remembrance in the face of overwhelming darkness.

The Final Days

The narrative of the final days for the Frank sisters is a somber reflection of their journey from the hidden sanctuary of the Secret Annex to the grim realities of Bergen-Belsen, a stark contrast to their earlier life in Frankfurt filled with hopes and dreams. On October 28, a grim selection process began, identifying women to be transferred to Bergen-Belsen, another concentration camp. Among the more than 8,000 women chosen were Anne and Margot Frank, along with Auguste van Pels. Tragically separated from her daughters, Edith Frank was left behind, ultimately succumbing to the brutal conditions of disease, starvation, and exhaustion. Her life ended in January of 1945 at only 44 years, a victim of the cruel Nazi regime.

Upon the arrival of the Frank sisters and others at Bergen-Belsen, the camp struggled to accommodate the sudden surge of prisoners. Hastily erected tents became their shelters, yet these were insufficient as diseases, particularly typhus, ravaged the overcrowded conditions. The onset of winter in 1944 further transformed Bergen-Belsen into a harrowing landscape of suffering. The camp's severe overcrowding and virtually nonexistent hygiene facilitated the rampant spread of deadly diseases. The prisoners were deprived of basic necessities such as food, sanitation, beds, or even adequate shelter, forcing them to lie on mere straw over the cold, damp earth, barely protected from the elements.

Amidst this despair, a poignant moment of human resilience shone through when Rebekka Brilleslijper, later known as the artist Lin Jaldati, and her sister Jannie, who had befriended the Frank girls back in Westerbork, were reunited with them. Despite the grim circumstances, their encounter symbolized the enduring spirit of hope. However, the dire conditions in the camp took a toll on Anne and Margot's health, leading to a significant decline due to malnutrition and the brutal camp regimen. The sisters faced these trials together, their bond a glimmer of light in the darkness.

A severe storm soon after their arrival wreaked havoc on the camp, damaging many tents, including the one sheltering the Frank sisters and the Brilleslijper sisters. This event left many displaced and exposed to harsh conditions, either beneath overturned tents or in makeshift shelters like sheds. The aftermath saw efforts to reorganize the camp, leading to the overcrowded modification of barracks in the star camp. Original two-tiered bunks were replaced with cramped three-tiered ones, further exacerbating the living conditions. The changes resulted in even more dire overcrowding, with irregular and insufficient food distributions, a scarcity of drinking water, and a complete neglect of hygiene by the camp authorities. Through this narrative, the final days of the Frank sisters at Bergen-Belsen are framed not just by the atrocities they endured but also by the moments of human connection and resilience against the background of unthinkable hardship.

In this bleak setting, Anne experienced a fleeting reunion with two old friends, Hanneli Goslar and Nanette Blitz, who found themselves trapped within the same barbed wire confines. Blitz, transferred to Anne's section in December 1944, and Goslar who was in the Sternlager since February of the same year, bore witness to Anne's deteriorated condition. Heartrending and poignant encounters with Blitz and Goslar offered a window into Anne's last moments, revealing a world apart from the one she once knew, filled with profound sorrow yet punctuated by fleeting moments of connection. Blitz recounted the shock of seeing Anne so thin and bald, a stark contrast to the vibrant girl she once knew. Despite her condition, Anne expressed a wish to transform her diary into a book after the war, a testament to her enduring spirit.

Goslar, in a gesture of compassion, attempted to provide care for the gravely ill Margot. Margot's condition had deteriorated to the point where she could not muster the strength to leave her bunk, a stark evidence of the severity of their plight. Anne, in these heartbreaking moments when her sister's condition was quickly deteriorating, revealed her belief that her parents were no longer alive to her friends, a thought that left the ever-vibrant Anne questioning the will to continue. These interactions, believed to have taken place in late January or early February 1945, sketch a portrait of fading hope and deepening despair among the sisters and their fellow inmates. Yet, despite the bleakness of their reality, the bond between Anne and Margot remained unbroken, witnessed by those around them as a profound tribute to their resilience.

Anne and Margot, weakened by malnutrition and the harsh conditions of camp life, fell even more ill. Their final days were marked by the struggle for survival in an environment that stripped away their dignity but could not diminish their bond.

Witnesses later recounted seeing the sisters together during these dire times, a testament to their unyielding connection amid despair. Margot, frail and debilitated, succumbed first to the typhus epidemic at the age of 19.
Only days later, Anne, then just 15 years old, also fell victim to the disease.

The exact dates marking the tragic end of Margot and Anne Frank's lives remain unchronicled, shrouded in the vast shadow of the Holocaust. For many years, it was believed that their deaths occurred in the bleak days leading up to the liberation of Bergen-Belsen by British forces on April 15, 1945. However, a reevaluation of historical evidence in 2015 suggests a far earlier demise, possibly as soon as February of that year. Witnesses reported seeing signs of typhus in the Frank sisters by February 7, aligning with medical insights that typhus victims often succumbed within 12 days after the beginning of symptoms. Further authenticating this timeline, Hanneli Goslar recalled that her father, Hans Goslar, passed away a week or two following their poignant meeting through the camp's barbed wire – a meeting that occurred shortly before Hans's death on February 25, 1945.

This chapter in the grim narrative of the Holocaust underscores not only the individual tragedy of the Frank sisters but also the collective fate of the Jews deported from the Netherlands. Of the 107,000 Jews sent away between 1942 and 1944, a mere 5,000 survived the war's atrocities. Back in the Netherlands, around 30,000 Jews evaded deportation with the aid of the Dutch underground, two-thirds of whom survived to witness the war's end. This stark contrast in survival rates depicts the merciless efficiency of the Nazi extermination campaign and the slender threads of hope and resistance that persisted in the face of overwhelming darkness.

Otto Frank, the sole survivor among the eight people who hid in the Secret Annex, was liberated from Auschwitz by Soviet troops in January 1945. In the post-war calm of a city still nursing its wounds, Jan and Miep Gies offered him refuge as he began the heart-wrenching search for his family. The sorrowful news of his wife Edith's passing reached him during his journey, yet hope for his daughters' survival lingered. However, weeks later, that hope was extinguished with the confirmation of Margot and Anne's deaths in Bergen-Belsen.

In the aftermath, Otto sought to uncover the destinies of his daughters' friends, uncovering their stories of tragedy and survival. He learned of Sanne Ledermann, frequently mentioned in Anne's diary, who had perished in the gas chambers with her parents. Contrastingly, Barbara Ledermann, Margot's close companion, had miraculously survived the war's brutality. As Otto pieced together the fates of those who once filled the sisters' lives, he found solace in the survival of several school friends and the extended Frank family members who had escaped Germany in the mid-1930s, finding sanctuary in Switzerland, the United Kingdom, and the United States.

Miep Gies, one of the valiant helpers who had supported the family during their time in hiding, presented Otto with Anne's diary – a legacy of his youngest daughter's spirit and dreams. The diary, filled with Anne's observations, hopes, and reflections, became a symbol of resilience and a poignant narrative of a life cut tragically short. Otto's decision to fulfill Anne's dream of becoming a published writer led to the diary's publication, allowing her voice to resonate across generations and bear witness to the horrors of the Holocaust.

The Diary Lives On

In the aftermath of World War II, Otto Frank had been given a profound gift by Miep Gies – Anne's diary and a collection of her writings. It was unknown to Otto that Anne had meticulously documented their life in hiding. Upon reading her words, Otto encountered the depth of Anne's introspection and dreams for the first time, revealing a side of his daughter that was previously unseen. This revelation, alongside Anne's expressed desire to become an author, sparked in him a resolve to publish her diary. Otto talked about how discovering the diary was an eye-opening experience for him. Along with how the depth and intensity of his daughter's reflections were something he hadn't realized before. He mentions how these were aspects of her inner world that she never shared with anyone. This insight, alongside her articulated dream of becoming a writer, inspired him to think seriously about publishing her work.

Anne's diary initially served as a personal outlet for her thoughts, a secret she intended to keep from the world. However, inspired by a radio broadcast from Gerrit Bolkestein, a Dutch government official in exile, Anne was motivated to prepare her diary for potential publication, aiming to contribute to the historical record of the German occupation. Anne expanded her original diary with additional notebooks and loose papers, adding depth and breadth to her narrative. To maintain privacy and perhaps add a layer of creativity, she assigned pseudonyms to those sharing the Secret Annex, as well as their supporters. The Van Pels family was transformed into Hermann, Petronella, and Peter van Daan in her writings, while Fritz Pfeffer was reimagined as Albert Düssell.

In this revised diary, each entry was tenderly addressed to "Kitty," a character from Cissy van Marxveldt's Joop ter Heul series, which Anne found particularly captivating. Otto Frank, in preparing his daughter's diary for its first audience, merged her initial entries, 'version A' with the more polished 'version B'. This process led to the creation of two versions of the diary, which Otto would later combine, respecting Anne's use of pseudonyms for others while reinstating his family's real names.

The path to publishing Anne's diary was met with initial resistance and setbacks. Historian Annie Romein-Verschoor, despite her efforts, was unable to find a publisher willing to take on the manuscript. However, the turning point came when her husband, Jan Romein, a respected historian in his own right, took up the cause. He wrote a compelling article titled "Kinderstem" ("A Child's Voice") for Het Parool, a significant Dutch newspaper. In his piece, Romein highlighted the diary's raw and powerful account of life under fascist rule, shedding light on the day-to-day horrors faced by those under

Nazi occupation. His perspective emphasized the diary's value not just as a personal story, but as a stark reminder of the atrocities of fascism.

This article succeeded where direct efforts had failed, sparking public and publisher interest in Anne's writings. The diary's eventual Dutch publication under the title "Het Achterhuis" (literally translated to "The House Behind" but commonly known as "The Secret Annex" in English editions) in 1947, became a significant moment in literary history. It marked the beginning of Anne Frank's legacy as an author, ensuring her voice would not be silenced by her tragic death.

The diary's international reception varied initially, facing rejections in some countries while achieving significant success in others, notably in Japan, where Anne's narrative touched a deep chord. The publication of *Anne Frank: The Diary of a Young Girl* in the United States in 1952 met with positive reviews, predicting the diary's future as a pivotal historical and literary work.

The diary inspired a play by Frances Goodrich and Albert Hackett, which made its debut in New York City on October 5, 1955. This adaptation went on to receive the Pulitzer Prize for Drama, acknowledging its profound impact on the theatrical world. The success of the play led to the creation of a film titled "The Diary of Anne Frank" in 1959, which garnered both critical acclaim and commercial success. Biographer Melissa Müller noted that this dramatization played a significant role in shaping perceptions of Anne's story, making it more romantic and universally relatable. As the years passed, Anne Frank's diary gained remarkable popularity, becoming a staple in educational curricula across the United States and beyond. This inclusion in school programs has ensured that successive generations continue to learn about Anne Frank, her life, and her enduring legacy.

Following the diary's rise to prominence in the late 1950s, doubts and criticisms about its authenticity began to surface, initially in Sweden and Norway. In 1957, "Fria ord," a publication associated with Sweden's neo-fascist group, delved into controversial territory with an article by Harald Nielsen, a writer previously criticized for his antisemitic (jew-hating) commentary, especially against the Danish-Jewish author Georg Brandes. Neo-fascism, the ideology behind the magazine, sought to revive fascist principles, often characterized by extreme nationalist, authoritarian, and racially discriminatory beliefs, adapting them to contemporary contexts. Within this ideological framework, Nielsen's article challenged the authenticity of Anne Frank's diary, baselessly alleging it was the work of Meyer Levin, an American writer, rather than the real experiences of a young Jewish girl during the Holocaust. This claim, devoid of evidence, sought to undermine the historical significance of the diary and Anne Frank's legacy, reflecting the broader antisemitic and revisionist tendencies inherent in neo-fascist movements.

In 1958, during a Vienna performance of "The Diary of Anne Frank," a significant moment of controversy emerged. Simon Wiesenthal, a renowned Holocaust survivor and Nazi hunter, was confronted by a group of protesters who denied the very existence of Anne Frank, claiming she was a fictional character made up by someone. This confrontation propelled Wiesenthal into action, leading him on a journey to validate Anne's life and the authenticity of her diary. His search reached its culmination in the discovery of Karl Silberbauer, the Gestapo officer directly involved in the arrest of the Frank family. When found, Silberbauer not only admitted his role in the arrest but also recognized Anne Frank from photographs, providing a firsthand account that verified the historical accuracy of the diary's events. This pivotal moment accentuated the diary's truthfulness against rising waves of denial and skepticism.

The controversy surrounding the diary's authenticity led to several legal challenges aimed at safeguarding its integrity. In 1959, Otto Frank took decisive legal action against Lothar

Stielau, a school teacher and former Hitler Youth member who had publicly denounced the diary as a fake and forged up. The legal challenge broadened to also include Heinrich Buddegerg, another individual who supported Stielau's claims through a letter published in a local newspaper. In response, a meticulous judicial examination was conducted in 1960, scrutinizing Anne's handwriting within the diary against other known samples of Anne's writing. This examination confirmed the diary's authenticity, leading to the court's official declaration of its genuineness. Following this judicial validation, Stielau retracted his accusations, and Otto Frank, having defended his daughter's legacy, chose not to pursue the case further.

Further attempts to discredit the diary came from Heinz Roth and Ernst Römer, who labeled the diary a forgery in separate publications. Legal action by Otto Frank led to convictions against both men, emphasizing the diary's authenticity. Throughout his lifetime, Otto was resolute in defending the integrity of the diary. He passed away from natural causes in 1980 in Switzerland at 91 years of age, having seen the diary withstand numerous unfounded claims against it. After his death, the diary and related materials were transferred to the Dutch Institute for War Documentation. A meticulous forensic analysis in 1986 by the Netherlands Ministry of Justice confirmed the diary's authenticity, examining the handwriting, paper, glue, and ink, with findings published in a "Critical Edition."

The 1990s saw continued efforts by Holocaust deniers to undermine the diary's accuracy. A notable instance involved Robert Faurisson and Siegfried Verbeke publishing a critical booklet. Legal actions by the Anne Frank House and Anne Frank Fonds, two organizations committed to preserving Anne Frank's legacy, sought to prevent the distribution of denial literature in the Netherlands. The Anne Frank House, a museum located in the actual building of the Secret Annex where Anne and her family hid, focuses on educating the public about the Holocaust and promoting human rights. The Anne Frank Fonds, established by Otto Frank in Basel, Switzerland, manages the copyrights of Anne's diary and supports educational projects worldwide. These efforts led to a 1998 court ruling that enforced the diary's authenticity and penalized further dissemination of denial literature, reinforcing the historical truth of the Holocaust. Through these challenges and affirmations, Anne Frank's diary has transcended its initial private purpose to become an enduring symbol of resilience against oppression.

Moreover, since its initial publication, the diary has seen the inclusion of content previously omitted by Otto Frank and editors, enriching its depth and authenticity. This new material, integrated into editions post-2001, after a resolution of copyright disputes, illuminates Anne's candid explorations of her emerging sexuality, reflections on her body, and her musings on menstruation – topics Otto had originally excluded for their personal nature or due to societal norms of the time. Moreover, pages that Anne herself had covered were uncovered and deciphered in 2018, revealing her musings on sex education alongside some light-hearted, 'dirty' jokes, showcasing her youthful curiosity and humor.

This additional content not only provides a fuller picture of Anne as a thoughtful, maturing individual but also underscores the universal aspects of adolescence. The revelations about her parents' marriage and her complex relationship with her mother offer a more in-depth view of family dynamics in the Secret Annex, highlighting the strains and challenges alongside moments of affection and mutual support. These expanded editions bridge the gap between Anne's experience and that of readers today, demonstrating the timeless relevance of her reflections and the enduring power of her voice. Through these unfiltered entries, readers gain a more intimate understanding of Anne's inner world, her intellectual and emotional growth, and the extraordinary circumstances under which she matured.

Anne Frank's diary, through its publication, controversies, and eventual vindication, stands as a testament to the enduring power of a young girl's voice against the backdrop of war. Its journey from hidden pages to global recognition underscores the universal resonance of Anne's insights and dreams, connecting generations to the legacy of hope and resilience she left behind.

Legacy and Memory

The legacy of Anne Frank extends far beyond the pages of her diary; it's a story that has been cherished, debated, and preserved across decades. In May 1957, stimulated by the initiative of Otto Frank and a group of dutiful citizens, the Anne Frank Stichting was founded with a poignant mission: to save the Prinsengracht building, the hiding place that harbored the Frank family and others from Nazi persecution, from demolition. Their efforts culminated in the opening of the Anne Frank House as a museum on May 3, 1960, inviting the world into the silent witness of Anne's life in hiding. The museum, though unfurnished to allow visitors an easy and uninterrupted passage through the historical rooms, holds sacred the remnants of its past occupants.

Within the hallowed walls of the Anne Frank House are fragments of daily life that breathe life into the story of the Frank family and their time in hiding. Among these are the reminders of Anne's youthful enchantment with the glamor of movie stars. These photographs of movie stars were carefully glued by Anne onto the walls of her confined space, serving not just as a window to a world of dreams and fantasy but also as an expression of her longing for the life outside that was brutally denied to her.

Similarly moving is the section of wallpaper where Otto Frank diligently marked the heights of Anne and Margot as they grew up in hiding. Furthermore, the map on the wall, annotated by Otto to track the advance of the Allied Forces, stands as a symbol of hope amidst despair. It reflects the family's clinging to the prospect of liberation, their hopes pinned on the shifting tides of a war that had taken so much from them. This map, protected behind acrylic glass for safety, speaks volumes about the resilience and unyielding spirit of those who, even in the darkest of times, dared to dream of freedom and a return to peace. The personal relics, now preserved behind acrylic for visitors to behold, offer a tangible connection to the lives of those who dwelled within the Annex.

From Peter van Pels' tiny room, a corridor now leads to the adjacent buildings, also acquired by the Foundation. These spaces serve not only to safeguard Anne's diary but also to host a variety of exhibits. These displays delve into Holocaust history and explore issues of racial intolerance in today's world. This museum, one of Amsterdam's top attractions, welcomed an average of 1.2 million visitors annually from 2011 to 2020.

Not far from this solemn remembrance site stands a bronze statue of Anne Frank, crafted by Mari Andriessen, her figure captured in a moment of youthful optimism, a poignant contrast to the narrative her life unfolded. This statue, situated in a square and watched over by the towering windows of the surrounding buildings, serves as a constant reminder of the light of hope that darkness cannot overshadow.

In an effort to extend Anne's legacy beyond the confines of the museum, Otto Frank, alongside his second wife, Elfriede Geiringer-Markovits, established the Anne Frank Fonds in Basel, Switzerland, in 1963. This foundation not only safeguards the diary's copyright but also champions educational initiatives against racism. By lending Anne's papers to exhibitions like the one at the United States Holocaust Memorial Museum in 2003 and supporting projects worldwide, the Fonds strives to illuminate the darkness of prejudice with the enduring light of Anne's story.

In 1997, Frankfurt's Dornbusch neighborhood, once home to Anne Frank and her family, saw the initiation of the Anne Frank Educational Center. This establishment serves as a beacon of learning, inviting both the young and old to delve into the history of National Socialism and its lasting impact on the present day.

Not far from there, in Amsterdam, the Anne Frank School stands as a testament to her enduring legacy, along with the Anne Frank tree, a silent witness to history in the garden behind the Anne Frank House. Meanwhile, the Merwedeplein apartment, the Frank family's residence from 1933 until their hiding, was preserved and restored to its original 1930s condition after being featured in a documentary. This project, led by Teresien da Silva of the Anne Frank House and Anne's cousin, Bernhard "Buddy" Elias, now hosts a unique residency program for writers who are constrained in their home countries, offering them a sanctuary to express their thoughts freely. The initiative began with Algerian novelist El-Mahdi Acherchour, marking the apartment not just as a historical site but as a cradle of contemporary literary creation.

Anne Frank's story, a poignant narrative of hope, despair, and the human spirit's resilience, has been etched into the global collective memory, transcending borders and generations. In the Netherlands, her story is not just a chapter from the past but an integral element in the fabric of Dutch historical consciousness. Recognizing its profound significance, the Dutch government included Anne Frank's story in the canon of the Netherlands, a curated list of fifty themes that encapsulate pivotal moments and figures in Dutch history. This canon, introduced in 2006 and reaffirmed with updates in 2020, serves as an educational framework designed to guide the teaching and understanding of the nation's past.

In a heartening gesture of remembrance and preservation, "Buddy" Elias donated a treasure trove of 25,000 family documents to the Anne Frank House in June 2007. These artifacts, encompassing photographs and a letter from Otto Frank announcing the loss of his wife and daughters, serve as enduring links to the personal history of the Frank family, offering insights into their lives and the catastrophic period they had to endure.

The narrative of Anne Frank and her indomitable spirit finds resonance in educational settings and popular culture alike. The Anne Frank Educational Center in Frankfurt and the multitude of schools worldwide bearing her name underscore the global commitment to remembering her legacy and the lessons it imparts.

Films, plays, and numerous references across media have woven Anne's story into the fabric of collective memory, ensuring her voice, once confined to a hidden annex, echoes through time. Highlights include the performance of "The Anne Frank Ballet" by Adam Darius in 1959, the vocal compositions "Annelies" in 2005, and "The Beauty That Still Remains" by Marcus Paus in 2015. The only visual memory of Anne, a silent film clip from 1941 showing her watching a wedding, remains a touching reminder of her brief life. This footage, donated to the Anne Frank House by the wedding couple who survived the war, offers a rare glimpse of her in a moment of everyday curiosity.

Anne's impact reached global recognition when Time magazine, in 1999, included her among the century's most influential heroes and icons for her courage and powerful narrative. Novelist Philip Roth described her as Franz Kafka's "lost little daughter," a tribute to her literary significance and tragic fate. In a tribute to her lasting influence, Madame Tussauds introduced a wax figure of Anne in 2012, and an asteroid discovered in 1942 was named "5535 Annefrank" in her memory, immortalizing her contributions to humanity's struggle against tyranny and oppression.

With over 270 schools named after her, from Germany to the United States and beyond, Anne Frank's legacy is not just about looking back at the horrors of the past but also about inspiring future generations. It's a call to remember the fragility of freedom, the perils of hatred, and the enduring strength of the human spirit to rise above despair. As new memorials are erected and her story finds new avenues of expression, Anne Frank remains a bringer of hope and a reminder of the power of a single voice to alter the course of history.

The Betrayal of the Frank Family

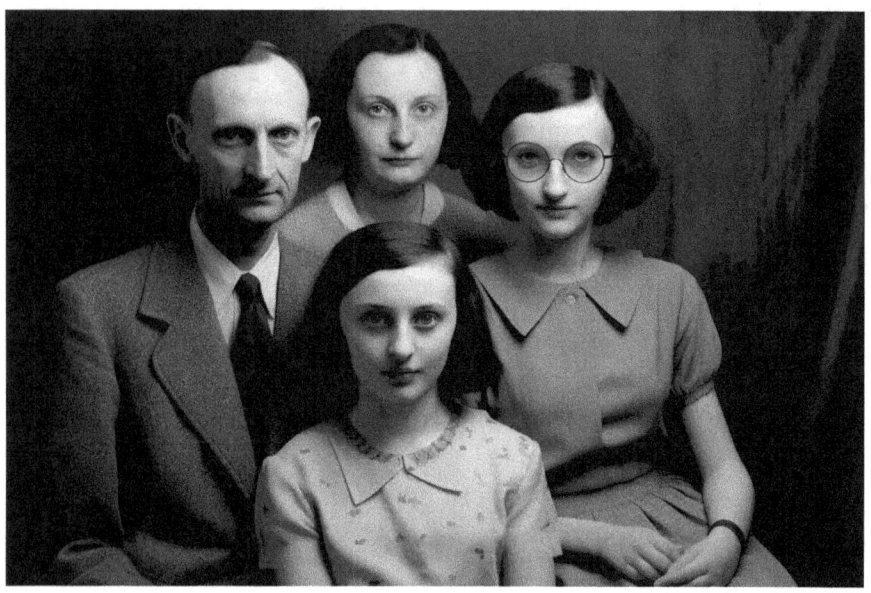

In the aftermath of World War II, amidst the countless tales of bravery and tragedy that emerged, the story of Anne Frank and her family stands out, not just for their courage but also for the enduring mystery surrounding their betrayal. The question of who betrayed the Frank family to the Nazis is a haunting enigma that has stirred both academic inquiry and public fascination for decades. Over the years, various theories have been proposed, each adding layers to this complex historical puzzle and reflecting the intricate interplay of human motivations under the oppressive shadow of tyranny.

Central to one of these theories is the Voskuijl family, with a particular focus on Nelly Voskuijl. Allegations of her Nazi affiliations present a stark contrast to her family's efforts to protect the Franks, casting a long shadow over their heroic actions. The biography by Flemish journalist Jeroen De Bruyn and Joop van Wijk, Bep Voskuijl's youngest son, claims that Nelly, involved in her youthful romance with Nazi ideology, might have been the one to betray the Franks. This proposition adds a profound layer of complexity, shedding light on the war's capacity to divide families and test loyalties to the breaking point.

Nelly's story, characterized by her alleged involvement with the Nazis and subsequent ideological conflicts with her family, particularly her sister Bep and their father, Johannes Voskuijl, is a vivid illustration of the moral and existential dilemmas that the war imposed on individuals and families alike. Johannes, the craftsman behind the secret bookcase door that concealed the Frank family's hiding place, and Bep, a steadfast supporter of the hidden Jews, found themselves at odds with Nelly's alleged Nazi sympathies. These internal family conflicts reflect the broader societal divisions wrought by the war, highlighting the complex web of relationships and allegiances that formed the backdrop to the Franks' betrayal.

Another theory, explored by the Anne Frank House, suggests that the raid leading to the Frank family's arrest could have been sparked not by a deliberate act of betrayal but by an investigation into ration card fraud. This perspective introduces an element of tragic coincidence to the discovery of the Franks, suggesting that their fate may have been sealed by the chaotic circumstances of the time rather than by the malicious intent of an individual. It broadens our understanding of the dangers faced by Jews in hiding, emphasizing that the threat of betrayal was just one of many dangers in a landscape filled with danger and uncertainty.

The speculation surrounding Ans van Dijk, a Jewish woman who infamously collaborated with the Gestapo, the official secret police of Nazi Germany, adds another dimension to the narrative of betrayal. Van Dijk's role in the capture and demise of numerous Jews is a chilling reminder of the Holocaust's capacity to compel individuals to commit acts of profound betrayal. Her potential involvement in the Frank family's fate is a vivid example of the tangled network of collaboration and resistance that characterized life in the occupied Netherlands, further complicating the search for the betrayer.

"The Betrayal of Anne Frank: A Cold Case Investigation" emerged as a pivotal addition to the discourse on Anne Frank's story, igniting widespread debate and controversy upon its publication. Authored by a team led by Canadian investigator Vince Pankoke, the book represented an ambitious attempt to apply modern investigative techniques to one of the most enduring mysteries of the Holocaust: the betrayal of Anne Frank and her family. Utilizing a combination of cold case investigative methods, historical research, and data analysis, the team sought to shed new light on the circumstances leading to the arrest of the Frank family.

At the heart of the book's claims was the assertion that Arnold van den Bergh, a member of Amsterdam's Jewish Council, could have been the informant who disclosed the Frank family's hiding place to the Nazis. This theory was presented as a conclusion drawn from an extensive review of historical documents, witness testimonies, and a detailed examination of the social and political landscape of Nazi-occupied Amsterdam. The investigators posited that Van den Bergh, facing immense pressure and the dire threat to his own family, may have made the harrowing decision to betray the Franks in an attempt to secure the safety of his loved ones and his family.

The book's publication was met with a mix of intrigue and skepticism and sparked intense discussion among scholars, historians, and the general public. Critics of the book questioned the reliability of its evidence and the validity of its conclusions, arguing that the investigation relied too heavily on speculative connections and circumstantial evidence. Prominent Holocaust scholars and experts in the field raised concerns about the methodology employed by the investigative team, suggesting that the book's claims lacked the clear validation required to support such a significant accusation.

As we continue to grapple with these theories and counterarguments, the definitive truth behind the betrayal of the Frank family remains elusive and unclear, obscured by the passage of time and the complexities of human behavior during wartime. The enduring quest to identify the betrayer, if such an individual existed, is a testament to the lasting impact of Anne Frank's story. It is a powerful reminder of the need to remember, to seek understanding, and to learn from the past.

The investigation into who betrayed the Frank family not only captivates our imagination and scholarly interest but also serves as a reminder of the complexities of human nature. It highlights the consequences of choices made under distressing situations, the fragility of trust in times of crisis, and the importance of historical remembrance. As new theories emerge and are scrutinized, the discourse surrounding this mystery enriches our comprehension of the Holocaust, prompting reflection, discussion, and a deeper appreciation for the nuanced layers of history.

The Holocaust: Beyond the Secret Annex

In crafting a narrative that goes beyond the walls of the Secret Annex to explore the broader experience of Jewish families during the Holocaust, it's crucial to begin by recognizing the unique and diverse stories that define this period. While Anne Frank's diary offers a deeply personal glimpse into life in hiding, it is but one of countless narratives that unfold against the landscape of one of history's darkest times. The Holocaust, a systematic campaign of extermination carried out by the Nazis and their collaborators, claimed the lives of six million Jews. Behind this staggering number lie stories of resilience, sorrow, and the indomitable spirit of those who faced unimaginable persecution.

The onset of the Nazi regime's rise to power in Germany marked a turning point for Jews throughout Europe. Anti-

Semitic laws, including the infamous Nuremberg Laws, stripped Jews of their rights, livelihoods, and dignity, setting the stage for the horrors that would follow. Families were uprooted from their homes, subjected to ghettoization,[1] and faced with the brutal realities of life under Nazi oppression. The ghettos, overcrowded and sealed-off sections of cities like Warsaw, Lodz, and Vilnius, became sites of severe deprivation and suffering, where disease and starvation were rampant.

As the Final Solution – the Nazi plan for the extermination of the Jews – was set into motion, families were torn apart, deported to concentration and extermination camps across occupied Poland and beyond. Auschwitz-Birkenau, Treblinka, Sobibor, and Belzec stand as grim testaments to human cruelty, their names synonymous with the systematic murder of millions during the Holocaust. These sites were not merely prisons but extermination camps designed with the sole purpose of mass murder, primarily through the use of gas chambers.

At Auschwitz-Birkenau, the largest of the Nazi death camps, a complex of gas chambers and crematoria was built to accelerate the Final Solution – the Nazis' plan to annihilate the Jewish people. Families who had survived the deplorable conditions of ghettos and forced labor camps found themselves facing unimaginable horrors. Upon arrival, they were subjected to a selection process. Those deemed unfit for work – mostly children, women, the elderly, and the sick – were immediately sent to the gas chambers. Disguised as showers, these chambers used Zyklon B, a cyanide-based pesticide, to

---

1. Ghettoization refers to the process by which the Nazis confined the Jewish population into designated areas of cities or towns called ghettos. These ghettos were often enclosed districts that isolated Jews from the non-Jewish population and from other parts of the city. The ghettos were exemplified by overcrowding, poor living conditions, lack of sanitation, and insufficient food. Life in the ghettos was extremely difficult, with many people dying from disease, starvation, or the harsh conditions, while others were later deported to concentration camps and extermination camps.

kill large groups of people quickly. The efficiency of this method was a horrifying hallmark of the Holocaust's brutality.

Treblinka, Sobibor, and Belzec, while smaller than Auschwitz, were no less deadly. These camps were part of Operation Reinhard, the code name for the plan to exterminate all Jews within the General Government district of Poland. Here, the Nazis refined their methods of mass murder, using gas chambers from the start. These camps operated with ruthless efficiency, and the vast majority of those deported to these camps were murdered upon arrival, their bodies buried in mass graves or burned to erase evidence of the crimes.

Life in these camps, for those few selected to temporarily survive, was marked by constant terror, starvation, and forced labor, all under the shadow of the gas chambers. The existence of these camps and the systematic extermination of Jews and other victims represent one of the darkest chapters in human history, highlighting the depths of hatred and the capacity for genocide.

In the shadow of the Holocaust's unimaginable horrors, instances of defiance and resilience illuminated the darkest times, offering glimmers of hope and human dignity. Among these, the Warsaw Ghetto Uprising of 1943 remains a powerful symbol of resistance against Nazi oppression. This act of rebellion stands as a towering symbol of the resilience and defiance of the human spirit in the face of the Holocaust's unspeakable atrocities. The uprising, which unfolded in the Warsaw Ghetto in Nazi-occupied Poland, marked the largest Jewish resistance effort against the Nazi regime during World War II. It wasn't merely a battle for survival, but a profound declaration of the intrinsic human desire for freedom and dignity under the shadow of imminent death.

The uprising began on April 19, 1943, coinciding with Passover[2], when Nazi forces entered the ghetto intending to

---

2. Passover is a significant Jewish holiday that commemorates the liberation of

deport the remaining Jewish population to concentration and extermination camps. By this time, the Warsaw Ghetto, once home to over 400,000 Jews, had been decimated through mass deportations to camps such as Treblinka. The Jewish resistance, aware of their fate, chose to stand their ground, refusing to be led silently to the slaughter.

The Jewish Combat Organization (Żydowska Organizacja Bojowa, ŻOB) and the Jewish Military Union (Żydowski Związek Wojskowy, ŻZW), composed mainly of young men and women, led the resistance. Despite being vastly outnumbered and outgunned, with only a cache of light weapons, homemade bombs, and Molotov cocktails at their disposal, these fighters managed to inflict significant damage on the German forces. Their resistance turned the ghetto into a battlefield, with barricades, hidden passages, and fortified positions.

For nearly a month, the fighters engaged in guerrilla warfare, using the ghetto's complex network of houses, cellars, and sewers to their advantage. The Nazis, surprised by the ferocity and determination of the resistance, were forced to retreat initially but returned with reinforced numbers and heavier weapons. The uprising was met with a brutal response; the Nazis systematically destroyed the ghetto, block by block, burning down buildings with flamethrowers, and killing or capturing the inhabitants.

The Warsaw Ghetto Uprising was ultimately quashed by mid-May 1943, with the destruction of the Great Synagogue of Warsaw on May 16 serving as a symbolic end to the rebellion. The majority of the remaining ghetto residents were killed in

---

the Israelites from Egyptian slavery, as described in the Book of Exodus in the Hebrew Bible. It is celebrated for seven or eight days (depending on the tradition followed), during which observant Jews refrain from eating leavened bread, using matzah (an unleavened bread) instead, to symbolize the haste with which the Israelites fled Egypt, leaving no time for their bread to rise.

the fighting or deported to concentration and extermination camps.

Elsewhere in Europe, similar stories of bravery unfolded as Jews joined or formed freedom fighter groups, engaging in guerrilla warfare against the Nazi regime. These fighters sabotaged railways, attacked German supply lines, and aided Allied intelligence efforts, all while living under constant threat of discovery and retribution. Their efforts not only disrupted Nazi operations but also served as crucial acts of resistance, preserving their humanity and agency in a time when both were relentlessly under attack.

The experience of children during the Holocaust, like Anne Frank's, highlights the particular vulnerabilities and resilience of the youngest victims. Hidden in attics, cellars, or in plain sight, disguised as non-Jews, many children lived with the constant fear of discovery. Others were smuggled out of ghettos and camps, finding refuge with non-Jewish families willing to risk their lives to save them. The Kindertransport, a rescue mission that brought thousands of Jewish children to safety in the United Kingdom, symbolizes both the desperation of the times and the capacity for humanity amidst cruelty.

In the Vilna Ghetto, amidst the relentless horrors of the Holocaust, a remarkable story of cultural resistance and preservation unfolded, spearheaded by the Paper Brigade. This group, composed of poets, writers, and scholars, embarked on a secret mission to save Jewish history and culture from the Nazis' systematic attempt to obliterate it. At immense personal risk, these individuals hid and protected thousands of manuscripts, books, and documents, ensuring the survival of centuries' worth of Jewish thought, tradition, and knowledge.

Under the guise of sorting through Jewish cultural items for the Nazis – who intended to use these materials for a museum of an extinct race – the Paper Brigade secretly set aside significant works. They buried texts in metal boxes and milk cans beneath the ghetto and in other secure locations, often under the cover of darkness, to evade detection. Their actions were a profound assertion of resistance against the Nazis' cultural genocide, preserving not only literature and religious texts but also scientific papers and works of art. The courage and foresight of the Paper Brigade highlight a significant aspect of resistance during the Holocaust: the struggle to maintain identity, memory, and cultural continuity in the face of systematic annihilation.

As the war came to an end and the full scope of the Holocaust was revealed, the surviving remnant of Europe's Jewish communities faced the daunting task of rebuilding their lives amidst the ashes of their former existence. For many, the return to life as it was before the Holocaust was impossible – families had been decimated, communities destroyed, and the trauma of their experiences indelibly marked on their memories.

Amidst this dark era, a number of individuals emerged from the depths of unimaginable despair to share their experiences with the world. Their stories of survival are not just records of historical significance but are profound narratives of human resilience, courage, and the indomitable spirit to overcome.

Elie Wiesel, a Romanian-born Jewish-American, survived the Auschwitz and Buchenwald concentration camps. His groundbreaking work, "Night," provides a haunting account of these experiences, examining themes of faith, identity, and familial bonds in the shadow of inconceivable horror. Wiesel's contributions as a professor, political activist, Nobel Laureate, and author have left an unerasable mark on our collective conscience, urging humanity to remember and learn from the atrocities of the Holocaust.

Another remarkable figure, Simon Wiesenthal, known for his relentless pursuit of justice, dedicated his life to tracking down

Nazi war criminals. Surviving several concentration camps, including Auschwitz, Wiesenthal became a famed Nazi hunter, aiding in the capture of individuals responsible for the Holocaust, thereby ensuring that justice served as a cornerstone of historical memory. After the war, he founded the Jewish Documentation Center in Vienna, which played a crucial role in gathering evidence against former Nazis. His efforts led to the arrest of numerous high-profile figures, including Adolf Eichmann, one of the architects of the Holocaust. Wiesenthal's work not only sought retribution but also aimed to educate future generations on the atrocities committed during World War II.

Italian Jewish chemist and writer Primo Levi, who survived Auschwitz, delved into the moral quandaries and philosophical debates borne out of the Holocaust. His works, notably "If This Is a Man," explore the profound impacts of the concentration camps on the human psyche, offering a raw and introspective look into the human condition under duress.

The narrative of resilience in the face of systematic extermination is further echoed in the stories of survivors like Roman Kent, Gerda Weissmann Klein, and Thomas Buergenthal. Kent, enduring the brutality of several camps, later emerged as a vocal advocate for Holocaust education and human rights. Klein's autobiography, "All But My Life," chronicles her survival through labor camps and a death march, while Buergenthal's "A Lucky Child" narrates his miraculous survival as one of the youngest inmates of Auschwitz and Sachsenhausen, and his subsequent contributions to international human rights law.

The story of Eva Mozes Kor is a profound example of the human capacity for forgiveness and the transformative power of reconciliation, even in the aftermath of unspeakable atrocities. Born in 1934 in Romania, Eva and her twin sister, Miriam, were only ten years old when they were deported to Auschwitz. There, they became part of a group of children subjected to the horrifying medical experiments conducted by Dr. Josef Mengele, infamously known as the "Angel of Death."

Despite the brutal treatment and the immense suffering they endured, Eva's post-war life took a path that many found astonishing – she chose to publicly forgive those who had persecuted her and her sister, along with all the Nazis for their crimes against humanity. This remarkable decision was not an easy one, and it was met with a mix of admiration and criticism within the survivor community and beyond.

In addition, Yisrael Kristal's life serves as a testament to the endurance of the human spirit, surviving Auschwitz to be recognized as the world's oldest man at 113 years of age and Holocaust survivor, before he passed away in 2017. Similarly, Edith Eger's transformation from Auschwitz survivor to renowned psychologist exemplifies the capacity for trauma to forge paths toward understanding and helping others.

Max Eisen's narrative, captured in "By Chance Alone," details his survival from the labor and medical experimentation at Auschwitz, shedding light on the personal loss and the journey toward recounting the horrors faced by his family and countless others during the Holocaust.

These survivors, through their lived experiences and subsequent advocacy, education, and literary contributions, have ensured that the lessons of the Holocaust continue to resonate. Their stories stand as pillars of hope, resilience, and the relentless pursuit of justice, serving as a solemn reminder of the atrocities humanity is capable of inflicting, and the enduring spirit to overcome, remember, and educate. The legacy of these families inflicted with the Holocaust, their suffering, and their resilience, continue to resonate today.

Museums, memorials, and educational programs around the world are dedicated to ensuring that the stories of Holocaust victims and survivors are not forgotten, serving as a solemn reminder of the depths of human cruelty and the enduring strength of the human spirit.

Reflections on Humanity and Hope

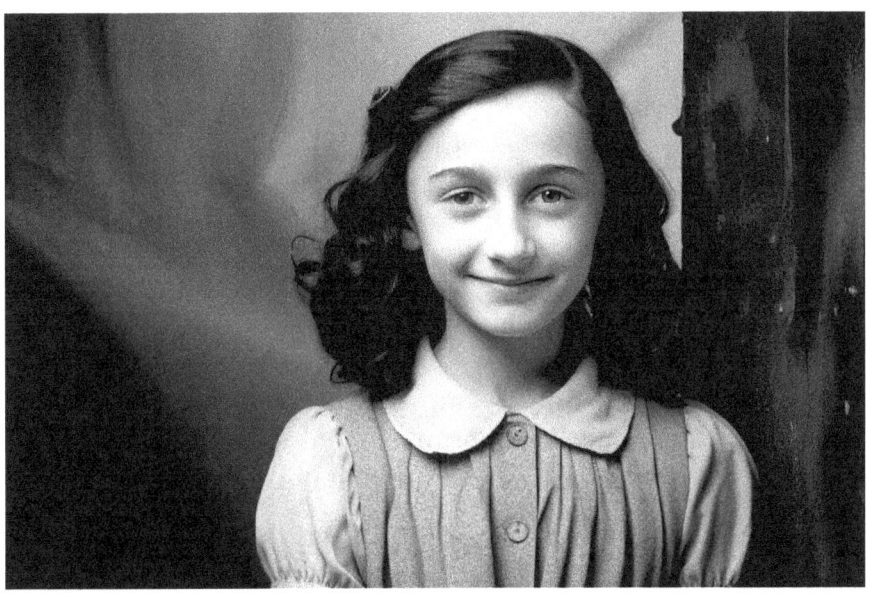

Amidst one of history's darkest hours, and a tragedy filled with millions, in the heart of Amsterdam, hidden behind a movable bookshelf, a young girl penned a diary that would become one of the most important symbols of human resilience and hope. The enduring legacy of Anne Frank's diary, with its introspective musings on humanity and unchanging optimism, has echoed through time, inspiring generations. It has been a catalyst for human rights advocacy, emboldened acts of bravery, and fostered a worldwide conversation on the pillars of peace and justice.

Within the cramped quarters of the Secret Annex, Anne found refuge in the written word, weaving narratives that were both profoundly personal and universally resonant. "I can shake off everything as I write; my sorrows disappear, my courage is reborn" she noted, capturing the essence of her diary as a sanctuary amidst the chaos of war.

Her reflections, imbued with a sense of introspection, dreams, and an unwavering faith in humanity, break through the barriers of time and place. Anne's perspective on life, encapsulated in entries such as, "Despite everything, I believe that people are really good at heart," has resonated with readers worldwide, inspiring them to look beyond despair and recognize the inherent goodness within others, even in the darkest of times.

Anne's musings on the potential for harmony and understanding among people serve as a poignant reminder of the individual stories behind the Holocaust's staggering toll. "How wonderful it is that nobody needs to wait a single moment before starting to improve the world," Anne wrote, her words echoing the sentiment that change begins with individual acts of kindness and understanding.

The diary's impact extends beyond a historical account of the Holocaust; it has inspired movements and individuals advocating for human rights and justice. The Civil Rights Movement in the United States, for example, found a symbol of hope and resistance in Anne's story. Leaders and activists, drawing parallels between the fight against racial segregation and the persecution faced by Jews under the Nazi regime, often cited Anne's faith in humanity to rally support for their cause.

Contemporary movements continue to be influenced by Anne's legacy, from global initiatives advocating for the rights of refugees fleeing persecution and conflict to campaigns combating anti-Semitism, racism, and discrimination in all its forms. Her diary has become a tool for education and empathy, encouraging individuals to stand up against injustice and to believe in the capacity for change.

The publication of Anne's diary in the aftermath of World War II came at a time when the world was grappling with the sheer scale of the atrocities committed. Her candid observations and unwavering hope inspired a wave of solidarity, encouraging individuals and communities to stand up against injustice and oppression. From the Civil Rights Movement in the United States to the fight against the racial segregation in South Africa, Anne's diary has been a moral compass, urging people to confront hatred with compassion and courage.

Anne Frank's reflections, penned with hope and a profound belief in the inherent goodness of people, have transcended the pages of her diary to ignite a global conversation on human dignity, rights, and the power of empathy. "Whoever is happy will make others happy too," Anne wrote, embodying her vision for a world steeped in mutual respect and joy. This simple yet powerful assertion has motivated human rights advocates, educators, and artists, propelling movements that seek to dismantle prejudice and champion the cause of the marginalized.

The Anne Frank House in Amsterdam stands as an everlasting witness to Anne's legacy and the Frank family's ordeal. Beyond preserving the history of those who hid within its walls, the museum has evolved into a vibrant educational hub. It offers programs like the "Free2choose" and "Let Me Be Myself" exhibitions, which encourage visitors to contemplate the importance of freedom and the consequences of its denial. By engaging with Anne's story, people from diverse backgrounds gain insights into the struggles faced by others, fostering a sense of solidarity and the impetus to act against injustice.

Anne's influence extends far beyond the museum. The diary has become a cornerstone of Holocaust education, helping students understand the catastrophic effects of racial hatred and the importance of standing against oppression. Her story has also found resonance in contemporary movements advocating for refugee rights and against xenophobia, which refers to fear, distrust, or hostility toward people from other countries, cultures, or ethnicities. Organizations have drawn parallels between Anne's experience as a refugee seeking safety and the plight of millions today, fleeing war and persecution. Her words, "I must uphold my ideals, for perhaps the time will come when I shall be able to carry them out," have inspired initiatives that aim to provide aid and advocacy for displaced populations, emphasizing the ongoing relevance of her hopes and dreams.

Moreover, Anne Frank's influence can be seen in global peace and justice efforts. The Anne Frank Peace Park, in Philadelphia, and the sapling from the chestnut tree Anne admired, planted at the United Nations Headquarters, symbolize her impact on international calls for harmony and understanding. These memorials remind us of Anne's longing for a peaceful world, urging us to contribute to the realization of this ideal in our communities and beyond.

In every mention of her name, every quote shared, and every story inspired by her diary, Anne Frank's voice continues to advocate for a world that chooses peace over conflict and justice over inequity. Her reflections on the dignity and worth of every individual challenge us to confront our prejudices and work tirelessly toward a society that honors the rights and contributions of all its members. Through education, advocacy, and the arts, Anne's legacy lives on, a light guiding us toward a future where tolerance and understanding bridge the divides.

Perhaps the most profound legacy of Anne Frank's diary is its embodiment of hope. Amidst the descriptions of daily life in hiding and the shadow of the Holocaust, Anne's belief in the goodness of people remains a powerful testament to her indomitable spirit.

Today, Anne Frank's diary is one of the most translated and widely read books in the world, an indication of its universal appeal and the global impact of Anne's story. It has been translated into over seventy languages, reaching readers in remote corners of the globe and continuing to inspire those who seek to make a difference. The diary not only keeps the memory of Anne Frank alive but also serves as a beacon of hope and resilience, reminding us of the strength found in vulnerability and the power of a single voice to effect change.

Conclusion

In the hidden confines of the Secret Annex, amidst the shadows of war and oppression, Anne Frank penned a diary that would emerge as a testament to the resilience of the human spirit. *A Brief History of Anne Frank* is not merely a narrative of hiding during one of history's darkest epochs; it's a journey into the heart of hope, courage, and the undying belief in the goodness of people, even in the face of overwhelming darkness.

Anne's words, written from the cramped quarters of her Amsterdam hideout, offer a window into the life of a young girl coming of age during the Holocaust. Her reflections, candid and profound, traverse the spectrum of human emotions – fear, love, despair, and hope. Amidst the setting of a world torn apart by war and hatred, Anne's diary is a powerful reminder of the light that can exist in the darkest of times.

The story of Anne Frank and her family is a chronicle of courage and survival. Forced into hiding to escape the Nazis' murderous regime, the Franks, along with four others, concealed themselves in the Secret Annex behind Otto Frank's business premises. For over two years, they lived in the constant shadow of discovery, relying on the kindness of friends for survival. Yet, it was within this confinement that Anne's voice flourished. Through her writings, she explored the complexities of her identity, the nature of human conflict, and her aspirations for the future. Her diary, initially a gift to document her thoughts and feelings, evolved into a profound narrative of her experiences and observations, reflecting a maturity far beyond her years.

Anne's reflections on humanity and hope are among the most compelling elements of her diary. Despite the persecution she and her family faced, Anne believed in the intrinsic goodness of people. She wrote, "In spite of everything, I still believe that people are really good at heart." This assertion, made amidst the horrors of the Holocaust, is a testament to her unbreakable spirit. It underscores her capacity to find hope in despair, to see beyond the immediate cruelty and suffering to a future where kindness and justice prevail.

The Frank family's story, though unique, is also a mirror reflecting the broader experience of Jews during the Holocaust. Across Europe, Jewish families faced unimaginable choices – whether to go into hiding, attempt escape, or confront almost certain death in the ghettos and camps. The diary provides a personal account among the universality of suffering, resistance, and survival that defined the Jewish experience during World War II. It serves as a bridge, connecting personal narrative to historical events, and offering insights into the daily realities of life under Nazi occupation.

The legacy of Anne Frank and her diary is an emblem of hope and a call to action. Anne's narrative transcends time and geography, resonating with new generations and inspiring countless individuals to stand against oppression. Her dream of becoming a writer was realized beyond her wildest imagination as her diary became one of the most important books of the 20th century. It not only serves as a historical document but as a source of inspiration for those who seek to make the world a better place.

In reflecting on Anne Frank's legacy, it is crucial to remember the context of her life and death. The Holocaust was a systematic attempt to exterminate the Jewish people, claiming six million lives. Anne Frank's story is a poignant reminder of the individuals behind the numbers, each with their own dreams, hopes, and stories. Her diary is a call to remember the past, to honor the memory of those who were lost, and to ensure that such atrocities are never repeated.

As we consider the reflections on humanity and hope within the pages of Anne Frank's diary, we are reminded of the power of a single voice to echo through the ages. Her words inspire us to look within and around us, to confront injustice, and to act with compassion and courage. Anne Frank's legacy is a manifesto of the enduring strength of the human spirit, a beacon of hope that continues to shine brightly in a world that, at times, seems overshadowed by darkness.

In conclusion, *A Brief History of Anne Frank* is more than a recounting of historical events; it is an exploration of the human condition, a meditation on the capacity for hope amidst despair, and a reminder of the impact one young girl's voice can have on the world. Anne's diary endures as a testament to the power of hope, the importance of remembering, and the unyielding belief in the goodness of people, even in the darkest times.

Appendix

This timeline offers a contextual background to the life of Anne Frank, illustrating how the turbulence of the time encapsulated her brief life.

1914

• The murder of Austrian Archduke Franz Ferdinand triggers the start of World War I, reshaping European politics and setting the stage for future conflicts.

1919

• Germany loses World War I. The Treaty of Versailles is signed, imposing harsh penalties on Germany and sparking protests and national resentment.

1925

• Adolf Hitler publishes "Mein Kampf," outlining his ideology of anti-Semitism and future plans for Germany.

1929

- Anne Frank is born on June 12, in Frankfurt am Main, Germany, into a world still recovering from the first global conflict and on the cusp of great upheaval.

1933

- Hitler and the Nazis come to power in Germany, marking a turning point that would lead to widespread persecution of Jews and other minority groups.

1934

- Seeking refuge from the increasing persecution in Germany, Anne Frank and her family emigrate to Amsterdam, signaling the start of a new life in a new city.

1936

- Hitler's first military action: German troops occupy the Rhineland, in violation of the Treaty of Versailles, as part of his aggressive expansionist policy.

1938

- The Kristallnacht, or "Night of Broken Glass," demonstrates the escalating violence against Jews in Germany. It becomes clear that Jews have no future under the Nazi regime.

- Fritz Pfeffer flees Germany for the Netherlands, escaping the growing persecution of Jews.

1939

- World War II begins as Germany invades Poland on September 1, leading to a global conflict involving most of the world's nations.

1940

- The Netherlands is drawn into World War II when Germany bombs Rotterdam and the country is forced to surrender, marking the beginning of occupation.

1941

- Mass raids take place in Amsterdam, leading to the first deportations of Dutch Jews to concentration camps, as part of the Nazis' Final Solution.

- The Dutch government, under German occupation, makes carrying an identity card compulsory, facilitating the tracking and persecution of Jews.

- Operation Barbarossa is launched as Germany invades the Soviet Union, opening the Eastern Front, which becomes one of the largest and deadliest theaters of war.

- Japan bombs Pearl Harbor on December 7, prompting the United States to enter the war after Hitler declares war on the US.

1942

- On June 12, Anne Frank receives a diary for her 13th birthday, a gift that becomes one of the world's most influential books, offering a poignant insight into life under Nazi occupation.

- By July 6, the Frank family goes into hiding in the Secret Annex behind Otto Frank's business at Prinsengracht 263 in Amsterdam, in an attempt to escape the Nazis' escalating persecution of Jews.

1942

- The Wannsee Conference in January marks the formalization of the "Final Solution," the Nazi plan for the genocide of the Jews, leading to the acceleration of deportations and mass exterminations across Europe.

1943

- The Warsaw Ghetto Uprising takes place in April, a significant act of Jewish resistance against Nazi efforts to transport the ghetto's remaining inhabitants to concentration and extermination camps.

1944

• D-Day, June 6: Allied forces land on the beaches of Normandy, France, marking a significant turn in World War II as they begin to push German forces back across Western Europe.

• In August, the hiding place of the Frank family and others in the Secret Annex is betrayed. They are arrested by the Gestapo and subsequently deported to concentration camps.

1945

• Edith Frank dies of starvation and illness in Auschwitz-Birkenau in early January, an indicator of the harsh conditions endured by prisoners.

• As the Soviet army advances, Auschwitz is liberated on January 27, but Anne and Margot have already been moved to Bergen-Belsen concentration camp in Germany.

• Anne and Margot Frank die of typhus in Bergen-Belsen, just weeks before the camp is liberated by British troops in April.

• World War II in Europe comes to an end with Germany's unconditional surrender on May 7.

• Otto Frank, the sole survivor of the Frank family, returns to Amsterdam in June and later learns of the deaths of his daughters and wife. He is given Anne's diary, preserved by Miep Gies, one of the helpers who supported the family during their time in hiding.

1947

• Anne's diary, *The Diary of a Young Girl*, is published in the Netherlands after Otto Frank decides to fulfill his daughter's wish to become an author. The diary offers a unique perspective on the daily life of Jews in hiding and becomes a seminal work in Holocaust literature.

1952

• The diary is translated into English and published as "Anne Frank: The Diary of a Young Girl," further expanding its reach and impact. The poignant reflections of a young girl caught in the horrors of war resonate with readers worldwide, making Anne Frank a symbol of the millions of lives lost during the Holocaust.

1960

• The Anne Frank House in Amsterdam is opened to the public as a museum dedicated to the memory of Anne Frank and the six million Jews who perished in the Holocaust. The museum not only preserves the hiding place but also serves as an educational center promoting human rights and combating anti-Semitism.

References

Abramson, Ann. *Who Was Anne Frank?* London. Penguin Books, 2007.

Frank, Anne. *The Diary of a Young Girl*. Toronto. Everyman's Library, 2010.

Gillian W, Perry. *Anne Frank's Legacy: How Her Story Changed the World*. HISTORYHIT (2023). https://www.historyhit.com/anne-franks-legacy-how-her-story-changed-the-world/ Accessed March 19th, 2024.

Müller, Melissa. *Anne Frank: The Biography*. New York. Bloomsbury Publishing. 2013.

Schwartz, Roy. *Opinion: The untold story about Anne Frank's hiding place*. CNN (2023). https://edition.cnn.com/2023/04/20/opinions/opinion-the-untold-story-about-anne-franks-hiding-place-schwartz/index.html Accessed March 10th, 2024.

Sinusoid, Darya. *Anne Frank: The Story of the Girl Behind the Diary*. SHORTFORM (2021). https://www.shortform.com/blog/anne-frank-story/ Accessed April 3rd, 2024.

Teague, Johnny. *The Lost Diary of Anne Frank*. Las Vegas. Histria Books, 2022.

Trouillard, Stéphanie. *80 years ago Anne Frank started her diary, a landmark of world literature*. France24 (2022). https://www.france24.com/en/europe/20220612-80-years-ago-anne-frank-started-her-diary-a-landmark-of-world-literature Accessed April 10th, 2024.

Thanks for reading!

As we close the final chapter of *A Brief History of Anne Frank*, I am grateful for the opportunity to embark on this personal journey with you through the pages of this book. Crafting this narrative has been a labor of love, driven by my deep reverence for Anne Frank's remarkable life and enduring legacy. Each chapter is a testament to my dedication to illuminating the complexities of her story and the profound impact it continues to have on our understanding of human resilience in the face of adversity.

This book transcends mere historical documentation; it is a heartfelt tribute to Anne Frank's indomitable spirit and the timeless relevance of her diary. Countless hours of research and reflection have gone into capturing the essence of her experiences, as well as the broader historical context in which they unfolded. Through meticulous attention to detail and narrative nuance, I have endeavored to bring Anne's world vividly to life, inviting readers to immerse themselves in her journey of courage, hope, and self-discovery.

Your feedback is invaluable to me, serving not only as a reflection of your own engagement with the text but also as a guiding light for future readers. Whether you found inspiration in Anne Frank's resilience, were moved by her poignant reflections, or have suggestions for how this work could be further enriched, I welcome your insights with an open heart and a deep sense of gratitude.

Please take a moment to share your thoughts and reflections through a review. Your voice has the power to shape the collective narrative of Anne Frank's legacy and to inspire others to embark on their own journey of discovery. Whether through a simple scan of the QR code provided or a few clicks of the mouse, your feedback is a vital contribution to our ongoing exploration of history's enduring lessons.

Thank you for joining me on this journey through the life and legacy of Anne Frank. May our shared appreciation for her story serve as a beacon of hope and understanding in an ever-changing world.

Warm regards,

Scott Matthews

Find more of my books on Amazon!

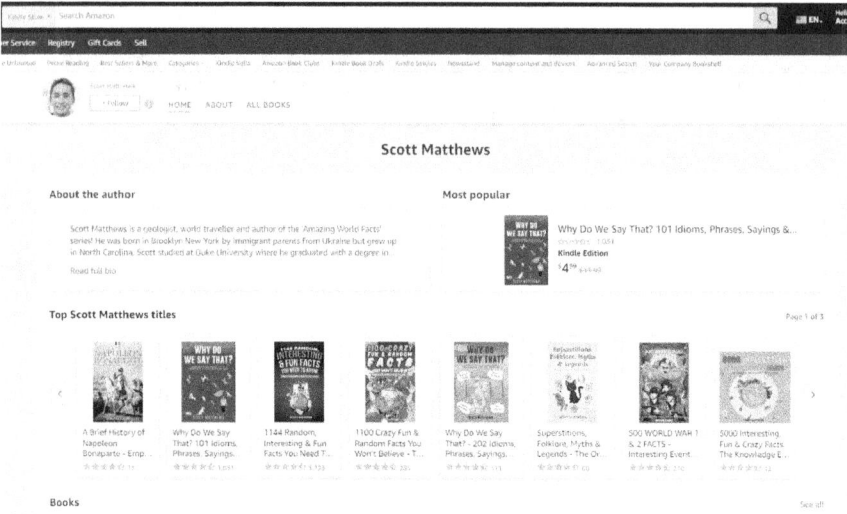

Discover more titles of the series "A Brief History of ..."!

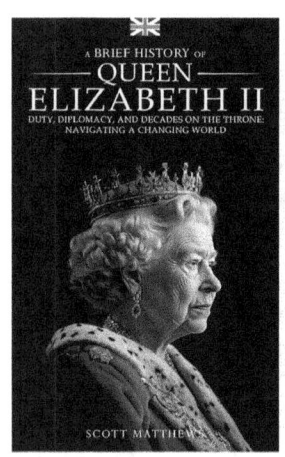

Explore the "Why Do We Say That" Series and Uncover the Origins of Everyday Idioms and Phrases

Bonus!

Thanks for supporting me and purchasing this book! I'd like to send you some freebies. They include:

- The digital version of *500 World War I & II Facts*

- The digital version of *101 Idioms and Phrases*

- The audiobook for my best seller *1144 Random Facts*

Scan the QR code below, enter your email and I'll send you all the files. Happy reading!

www.ingramcontent.com/pod-product-compliance
Lightning Source LLC
Chambersburg PA
CBHW072059110526
44590CB00018B/3233